THE SWEET CHESTNUT

The Sweet Chestnut

Linda & John Stanley

Publisher: Lizard Publishing
www.lizardpublishing.biz
info@lizardpublishing.biz
ISBN: 9780975011850 (print)
EISBN: 9780975011867 (ebook)
Printing and distribution:
Liing Source (USA, UK, AUS, EUR).

This book is dedicated to all the previous owners and their friends and family who owned Chestnut Brae and helped make it what is is today.

Contents

Dedication   v

Introduction   1

1 The Majestic Chestnut: A Tree Through Time   9

2 What is a Chestnut?   25

3 Chestnut as a Food ...historical significance   29

4 Chestnut - Breakfast   55

5 Chestnut - Starters   61

6 Chestnut - Sides   67

7 Chestnut - Main Course   77

8 Chestnut - Desserts   105

9 Chestnut - Drinks   131

About Chestnut Brae   139

Introduction

Linda Stanley in Chestnut Brae chestnut orchard in August

Once upon a time, Sweet Chestnuts were the major diet of many communities in Asia and Europe...but what do you do with them today?

The knowledge and wisdom from the past have been lost by many families. This included John and Linda Stanley when in 2013 they purchased Chestnut Brae, a sweet chestnut farm in Carlotta near Nannup in Australia's South West. Local farmers and chefs were mostly unaware of what to do with chestnuts, so John and Linda had to travel to Europe to seek the knowledge they needed for the development of their project. They met up and chatted with chestnut growers in Corsica and Italy to learn not only how they managed their chestnut orchards, but also how they added value to their crops and how their produce was marketed. Linda and John collected ideas for recipes and products that enabled them to start a new journey for Chestnut Brae.

Sweet Chestnuts are one of the oldest foods in the world, if not one of the first foods that humans actually ate. Chinese chestnuts are a species of chestnut *(Castanea mollissima)* native to China, Korea, and Taiwan and has been a staple food for centuries in that region. The European Sweet Chestnut *(Castanea sativa)* which is the variety of chestnuts on Chestnut Brae, originally came from Asia Minor. Castanea, which is the Latin name for the tree, is named after a small town in Turkey where it is believed the tree was discovered before being propagated and taken through Europe. There are chestnut trees in existence today that are known to be over 900 years old.

According to legend, a Greek army survived eating chestnuts while retreating from Asia Minor in 401 BC. When you consider chestnuts have twice the amount of starch as a potato one can understand why they were able to sustain an army.

The third species of sweet chestnut is the American chestnut *(Castanea dentata)* which was wiped out in the early 1900s by chestnut blight.

Linda and John worked with small farmers in the United Kingdom and North America teaching them how to retail and market their produce to the public. Agritourism and adding value to farm produce was an almost unknown concept in Australia at that time and Linda and John wanted to start the concept going so that they could give the "picture" to other small farmers in Western Australia. So, in 2011, Linda and John decided to purchase a small farm in Western Australia where they could create added-value products and develop agritourism.

Once they had purchased Chestnut Brae in 2013, they very quickly learned the historical importance, and significant health value of chestnuts, and felt it was important to show the world the various ways sweet chestnuts could be used in culinary dishes as it is one of the healthy superfoods of the world. That journey started in 2013 and continues today.

Extract from Hermann Hesse's "Narcissus and Goldmund"

"Outside the entrance of the Mariabronn cloister, whose rounded
arch rested on slim double columns, a chestnut tree stood close
to the road.

It was a sweet chestnut, with a sturdy trunk and a full round
crown that swayed gently in the wind, brought from Italy many
years earlier by a monk who had made a pilgrimage to Rome. In
the spring it waited until all the surrounding trees were green,
and even the hazel and walnut trees were wearing ruddy foliage,
before sprouting its first leaves; then, during the shortest nights
of the year, it drove the delicate white-green rays of its exotic
blossoms out through tufts of leaves, filling the air with an ad-
monishing and pungent fragrance.

In October, after the grape and apple harvests, the autumn wind
shook the prickly chestnuts out of the tree's burnished gold
crown; the cloister students would scramble and fight for the
nuts, and Prior Gregory, who came from the south, roasted them
in the fireplace in his room. The beautiful treetop—secret kin to
the portal's slender sandstone columns and the stone ornaments
of the window vaults and pillars, loved by the Savoyards and
Latins—swayed above the cloister entrance, a conspicuous out-
sider in the eyes of the natives.

Generations of cloister boys passed beneath the foreign tree, car-
rying their writing tablets, chanting, laughing, clowning, and
squabbling, barefoot or shod according to the season, a flower or
a nut between their teeth or a snowball in their fists.

There were always newcomers, and the faces changed every few
years, yet most of them resembled one another, if only for their
blond and curly hair. Some stayed for life, becoming novices and
monks; they had their hair shorn, donned habits and cinctures,

read books, taught boys, grew old, and died. Others after finishing their studies were taken home by their parents to castles, or merchants' and artisans' houses, and then went out into the world and lived by their wits or their crafts. They returned to the cloister occasionally as grown men, bringing their little sons to be taught by the priests, stood for a while smiling pensively at the chestnut tree, then vanished once more.

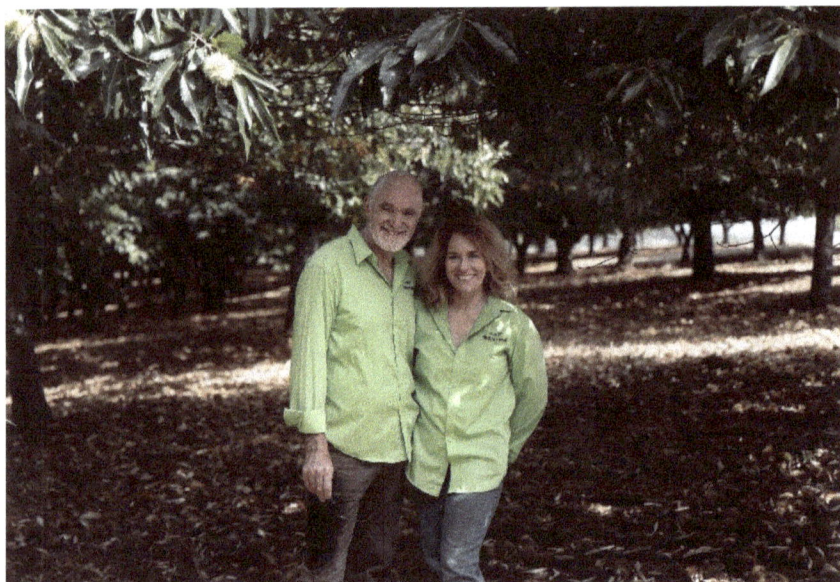

John and Linda Stanley in the chestnut orchard

Chestnut Brae

Linda and John Stanley purchased Chestnut Brae in October 2013. Although they had a passion for horticulture and spent their lives advising farmers and horticulturists on how to retail and market their produce, they had never owned a farm, so knew nothing about farming itself, and knew nothing about sweet chestnuts or how to grow them. They were well aware they had a lot to learn and, as they wanted to "save the planet" they did not want to use chemicals, but instead wanted to focus on natural and traditional methods. Knowing how depleted Australian soils are, their first focus was on building soil health.

Their passion and drive turned a rundown orchard into a thriving, award-winning, small business.

The first investment they made was to take a business trip to Corsica, France, and Italy, the home of the European sweet chestnuts, during the northern hemisphere harvest time to study how the crop was grown and harvested and to research how chestnuts were used in Europe and get ideas for recipes they could introduce on their own farm.

The most common questions from consumers in Australia are: -
    What is a sweet chestnut?
    What do you do with them?
    How do you cook them?
This book answers those questions.

1

The Majestic Chestnut: A Tree Through Time

A chestnut tree with young chestnut fruit

Imagine being born in Sicily in a village called Linguaglossa, located on the eastern slopes of Mt Etna, 8 km from the summit; every autumn you go and harvest sweet chestnuts.

Every year you would go to the biggest and oldest tree in the world, called Castagno dei Ceno Cavalli, and gather nuts. The whole village would forage enough chestnuts from this one tree to last them through the winter. This tree had a girth of 62 metres and is estimated to be 4,000 years old according to the Botanist Bruno Pevronel which means it was around when Plato was alive.

In the 19th century, the tree was recognised in the Guinness World Records as having the "Greatest tree girth ever."

The name of the tree, Castagno dei Ceno Cavalli, means "The Tree of a Hundred Horses." Legend has it that when the Queen of Aragon was in Sicily with 100 knights she was caught in a major thunderstorm, but the chestnut tree was so enormous that the whole 100 knights were able to take shelter under this tree.

Many believe the Sequoiadendron in California is the tallest tree, or the Methuselah bush or King's Holly, *Lomatia tasmanica,* in Tasmania is the oldest woody plant, but the sweet chestnut can beat them all.

The sweet chestnut is a member of the Beech family and is named after a village in Turkey, Kastanaia on the island of Oris Karvouni. This tree has had an interesting history in three regions of the world, namely America, China and Europe.

The Majestic Tree of the Appalachians

The American sweet chestnut, *Castania dentata*, in the 19th century, made up 50% of the trees growing in the Appalachian forests. Henry David Thoreau talked about *"the boundless chestnut woods"*. There is an old folklore saying in the USA that a squirrel could travel from Georgia to New York by jumping from chestnut to chestnut and its feet would never touch the ground.

In 1904 a bark fungus from the Far East, chestnut blight, *Endothia parasitika*, arrived via a Chinese chestnut imported to the New York Zoological Gardens. The disease spread quickly, and the chestnut forests began to die.

In 1911 legislation was introduced to save the chestnut trees and The Pennsylvania Chestnut Blight Commission was formed. However, there was little success. By 1940 nearly every tree had disappeared from the forests and with them went commercial chestnut growing in the USA. A few trees remain in Wisconsin, Oregon and California.

The American chestnut is a very close relative of the European chestnut (*Castanea sativa*) and therefore the European chestnut cannot replace the American chestnut as a commercial crop as the European chestnut is also prone to the Chestnut Blight disease.

The Iroquois Indians taught the Pilgrims how to grind chestnuts into flour and how to make a hot beverage that resembled coffee.

When Indians could not find birch for canoe making, they turned to chestnut as the timber of choice.

One of the chestnut family that is immune to the blight is a chestnut relative, Chinkapin, *Chrysolepis chrysophylla or Castanea pumila* which gets its name from the Indian word for chestnut. It is an evergreen tree that produces a small, sweeter version of nut that is mainly used as wildlife fodder, although you may sometimes see it at farmers' markets in the south of the USA.

Many chestnuts seen in retail stores in the USA now come from Europe. The chestnut industry is once more growing around Benton

Harbor and Ludington on the eastern shore of Lake Michigan, with research being carried out at the University of Michigan, but the production is less than 1% of the world's production.

Michigan is also the only State that grows a European x Japanese hybrid cultivar. At the time of writing, out of the 50 growers in the State, 32 are in a Growers Co-operative which was started in 2001. To date, this is the largest cooperative group of chestnut growers in the country and provides the market with 100 tonnes of nuts a year. The major focus is on selling fresh chestnuts between late September and December.

To become a member of the co-operative a grower must supply all their nuts not sold as farm gate sales and be able to supply a minimum of 5 tonnes of nuts to the market a year.

Growers grow the nuts and send them to a central processing unit where all post-harvest operations are gathered together. This leaves the grower to grow and the co-op to process and market. By being a co-operative, the co-op can invest in an Italian peeling unit, the only one in the USA and a FACMA harvesting unit. These facilities are shared between grower members of the co-op.

The cooperative policy is to provide "**Just in Time Fresh Chestnuts**" to retailers. On average, growers are getting twice as much return on their fresh nuts and have half the harvesting cost of many growers in Australia.

The "peak" body in the USA is Chestnut Growers of America which looks at national issues. Leading growers in the USA are closely watching what is happening in Chile. At the time of writing this book, large-scale planting of chestnuts is taking place in Chile, with most of the nuts from Chile being exported to Europe, but closer cooperation with the USA is a possibility.

A young chestnut orchard in Michigan USA

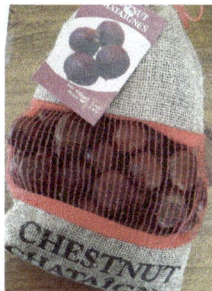

Chestnuts from
Italy in a store in
Ontario, Canada

Soap as a deer deterrent on a chestnut tree

One grower we met in Michigan uses soap as a deterrent to deer which chews the bark. Would this work with kangaroos that eat our nuts in Australia?

Largest Chestnut in the Americas

Ironically the largest chestnut in the USA is a European Chestnut planted in the 1880s by Battista Gianoli when he brought seed from Italy to the Gianoli Ranch in the Napa Valley in California. This tree is one of 47 he planted and in 1991 it entered the National Register of Big Trees. The tree is 73 feet (22.25 metres) tall with a branch spread of 78 feet (23.8 metres).

Keeping Trees Healthy

Compared to many plants, chestnuts do not suffer from many diseases or pests. The major problem is chestnut blight which destroyed the American chestnut forests.

Scientists in Australia have discovered a fungal fingerprint for a disease that cost Australia's chestnut industry more than $5m in 2016. The scientists discovered chemical markers for nut rot, which is internal and cannot be seen until the nut is opened. The nut rot fungus is *Gnomoniopsis smithogilvyi*. Humidity and moisture are the ideal conditions to encourage nut rot. The humid weather conditions encourage chemical compounds, called volatiles, to be released by the tree.

The Sweet Chestnuts of Asia

The chestnut is looked upon as the earliest nut used as a food in antiquity. Not only was it eaten, but the Chinese Emperor used it as a gift to his nobles.

Chestnuts grow in China, Korea, Taiwan and Japan. The Japanese Chestnut, *Castanea crenata*, is a small tree growing to around 10m in height. It is a prolific fruiting plant and the markets in Japan are full of nuts in season. In Japan, the tree is associated with success and hard times.

China has two species of chestnuts.

In the mountains of Huleh and Szechwan, you will find *Castanea henryi*, a tree that grows to around 20 metres in height. The Chinese Chestnut is *Castanea mollissima* and is widespread from Beijing to the far west. In China, the tree is a major source of fuel as well as nuts.

The Chinese enjoy the nut in all courses of a meal. Peking Wall is based on fresh chestnuts and cream, while Peking Dust is made from crushed chestnuts and cream.

The dead branches of chestnut trees in Japan are host to shiitake mushrooms which are also one of the world's healthiest foods.

Spanish Chestnut or Sweet Chestnut in Europe

Castanea sativa grows wild in Southern Europe, North Africa and Asia Minor and is believed to have been around for over two million years. It used to be believed the Romans introduced it into northern Europe including the British Isles where many would probably assume it is a native tree.

Recent pollen dating shows that the Celts were probably the people responsible for spreading the plant across Europe when they ate chestnuts with their wine.

Take a walk around Botanical Gardens in Europe and you will find various forms of the tree used as an ornamental park tree. 'Albo-marginata' is a variegated form, 'Asplenifolia' was a cut leaf form produced by the Loddiges Nursery in Middlesex, UK. 'Holtii' is a conical-shaped tree, 'Purpurea' has purple leaves in the spring, whilst 'Pyramidalis' is a pyramid-shaped tree.

The chestnut tree has become part of European folklore.

There are museums dedicated to the plant; in France at the Musée de la Châtaigneraie in Joyeuse, and in Italy at The Museo del Castagno in Val di Roggia, Lucca.

One of the most famous chestnut trees is Evelyn's Great Chestnut at Tortworth in Gloucestershire in the UK. This must be the most documented tree in the UK. The name Evelyn comes from John Evelyn who wrote about the tree in 1664. The tree was known as "The Old Chestnut of Tortworth" in 1150, suggesting it is over 1,000 years old. The tree was sketched in the 1712 book *"Ancient and Present State of Gloucestershire"* by Sir Robert Atkyns. Sir Robert describes a great chestnut that was around as a great tree during the reign of King John in the 13th century. By the 18th century, the tree was recognised as the oldest and largest tree in England. Although the debate has continued on the age of the tree, this wonderful tree is now estimated to be 1,100 years old, germinating in the reign of King Stephen.

The Tortworth Sweet Chestnut January 2019

Although an introduced tree to the United Kingdom, chestnut has become a tree of historical significance mainly because estate owners planted them as ornamental park trees.

Although many believe the "Evelyn" tree is the oldest in the UK, The Seven Sisters in Viceroy Wood in Kent has a plaque on it stating that this is the largest living tree in the British Isles. This sweet chestnut has seven limbs emerging from ground level. When it was last measured it had a girth of 15.5 metres and was 31 metres tall and around 1,000 years old. There is a debate on whether this is one tree or a group of seedlings that were "bundle planted" all those years ago.

Kateshill sweet chestnut tree

Kateshill Sweet Chestnut is 500 years old and is said to have the biggest spread of any chestnut in the UK. It is featured on the cover of "Heritage Trees", a book produced on the top 50 heritage trees in the UK.

Chestnut has its day in France. On St Martin's Day (11th November) chestnuts were distributed to the poor. The same occurred in Tuscany, Italy on St Simon's Day (October 28th).

Chestnut Festivals

Many towns in Europe have festivals based on chestnuts. In Portugal, they celebrate Dia de Sao Martnho or St Martin's Day on November 11th. St Martin of Tours was a soldier who became a bishop in the 4th century. In Portugal, they celebrate him with a bonfire, sweet chestnuts and a drink called jeripigo, which is a sweet fortified wine.

Goose & Chestnut Feast at Torrazzetta restaurant:

> "In Italy, the third weekend in October is the feast of goose and chestnuts, a typical tradition which calls for eating the goose, a symbol of abundance, in anticipation of the harsh winter which is approaching.
>
> The menu of the festival focuses on dishes with typical flavours of autumn, on the rediscovery of ancient traditions and the introduction of creative innovations, characterized by the presence of chestnuts and goose."

The Feast of Chestnuts

The chestnuts of Castione of Italy, a DOP product (Denominazione d'Origine Protetta - Protected Designation of Origin). The DOP label guarantees that the product is produced, processed, and packaged in a specific geographical zone and according to tradition) of the upland of Brentonico, are the protagonists of the "Feast of the Chestnut". A weekend in October is dedicated to food and wine with thematic menus and tastings.

> *"The Feast of the Chestnut"* is the perfect occasion to taste the chestnuts, but also typical dishes of Trentino, sweets and liqueurs made of them. *"Chestnut and wine: the excellent match."*

Sagra delle Castagne

One of the most spectacular Chestnut festivals is held every year in the village of Soriano nel Cimino, in late September. Soriano is around one hour north of Rome in the Tuscia, Maremma, Laziale region. The nearest large town is Viterbo. The region is a major sweet chestnut and hazel growing region and is home to FACMA the major machinery manufacturer in the chestnut industry globally.

The festival itself celebrates the Castagne (chestnut) as well as the patron saint, St George, as this is where St George killed the dragon. The event is held over three weekends and if you are into chestnuts this is the place to be at this time of the year.

Street decor celebrating St George at the chestnut festival Sagra delle Castagne in Soriano nel Cimino, Italy

Parade at the chestnut festival Sagra
delle Castagne in Soriano nel Cimino,
Italy

Chestnut Trails

We have been very fortunate to have been able to travel the chestnut
trails of Corsica and Italy.

One on our bucket list is The Chestnut Trail in Switzerland in the Ti-
cino hills from the Gulf of Agno on Lake Lugano to Monte Lema. Pic-
turesque Ticinese villages, narrow mountain lanes and vast chestnut
forests define the region, which is ideal for hiking and biking tours.
Tourists can visit shops to see the added value chestnut products. The
trail is sign-posted with the chestnut symbol. There are eight didactic
markers on this trail.

Hiking time: From Arosio 5-6 hours (Parking available), or from Fes-
coggia (Parkplätze vorhanden).

The Chestnut in Australia

Chestnut Orchard at Chestnut Brae

It is believed migrants introduced the European chestnut during the gold rush to the eastern states of Australia in the 1850s and 1860s. Some of these trees still exist in Victoria and are over 120 years old and 60 metres tall.

Today there are around 350 chestnut growers in Australia and the national yearly crop is around 1,200 metric tons with around 80% coming out of Victoria.

Our trees at Chestnut Brae were planted in the late 1970's. They were grafted European varieties, possibly on American seed stock, as we are told the grower, Werner Letert, imported seed from Oregon.

The old Olea Nursery catalogues (which supply young trees to the nursery industry in Western Australia) name the following chestnut varieties that were available at that time as being:

Brown Early. One of the earliest varieties available, reddish tinted skin, big nut, medium productively. Starts to drop in mid-March.

Morena. Very dark-coloured nuts (almost black) early maturing, heavy cropper. Vigorous growing trees. The nuts have a long-keeping quality. Ripens in mid-March.

Flat Mid-Season. Flat-shaped nuts, medium to small in size. Usual tree nuts on every burr. The trees tend to overproduce to the detriment of the vigour and size of the nut. Ripens in early April.

Autumn Bounty. This variety begins to fall in the middle of April and continues well into May. Large fruit with a typical chestnut colour. Easy to harvest and easy to peel. Excellent quality and consistent cropper.

Manjimup Mahogany. A local selection (probably from Fonty's Pool) By far the most beautiful looking fruit, dark shining skin with brown stripes, unusually shaped with a small base. The nuts begin to appear around the middle of April and they fall free of their burr, thus making harvest easy. Not a very heavy cropper, the largest of all the nuts.

(Information on varieties kindly supplied by Per and Helen Christensen, Ellendale Farm, Balingup, Western Australia)

2

What is a Chestnut?

Castanea belongs to *Fagaceae*, the beech tree family. The whole chestnut family have similar shaped leaves which makes the identification of the family easy, even if identifying species is more challenging. The flowers are unisexual and flower in spring or early summer. The catkins arise from young leaf axils. The lower catkins are the male flowers. Later leaf axils produce shorter female catkins which normally appear in clusters of two or three. Flowers are pale yellow and provide a distinct appearance to the tree when in full bloom. Although we find the aroma pleasant, many people have commented to us they find the aroma unappealing.

The nuts ripen in a prickly burr and most varieties eject the nut from the burr. The nuts are then harvested from the ground.

Chestnuts love hot summers and once established are drought-tolerant as long as the soil is well drained.

Traditionally plants are grown from seed or sucker, but modern varieties are grafted which is carried out at the seedling stage in the spring.

They prefer a soil pH of 6.5, the same as the oak and the hazelnut.

The Chestnut as a Timber tree

Chestnut wood is sturdy and relatively strong (80% that of oak) and hence is often called "the poor man's oak". The wood is full of tannin, a natural preservative, which means the wood has little sap and therefore is resistant to rotting, one reason the trees live so long. It is therefore a lumber tree, especially in Europe. The tree grows straight and therefore chestnut is used for many items. Everything from a telegraph pole to railway ties, floorboards, roof shingles, furniture and musical instruments.

The Chestnut Fence

When John was a lad in the UK, chestnut fencing was a common way of dividing properties. This type of fencing was a result of chestnut trees being coppiced for their timber.

Trees were pruned to ground level to allow for many young branches to emerge which would then be harvested every 10 to 25 years depending on the size of timber required.

Coppicing is rarely practised these days, but Stour Wood near Harwich in the UK still has a wonderful woodland of coppiced sweet chestnuts from 1675.

Coppiced UK woodlands are a wonderful place to visit when spring flowers are in bloom.

Wine Barrels

William Boutcher in his book written in 1778 entitled *"A Treatise on Forest-Trees"* mentions that in Italy chestnut was used for barrels for wine as when the wood has been seasoned it maintains its bulk without shrinking or swelling which most woods tend not to do. He also mentions that a lot of timber used to build London was also chestnut for the same reason.

Wood Chips for Smoking Food

Modern homeowners rarely use chestnut fencing but do light up the barbeque and at Chestnut Brae, we sell wood chippings of sweet chestnut to add flavour to smoked foods.

3

Chestnut as a Food ...historical significance

Chestnut Leaves

All parts of the sweet chestnut tree can be used, even the leaves.

O'Banon or Capriole Cheese is goats cheese wrapped in Sweet Chestnut leaves. It is an old French cheese whose popularity has been revived in the USA and was awarded the best cheese by the American Cheese Society in 2014.

Traditionally, chestnut leaves are used to wrap the cheese. The leaves are soaked in eau de vie. The tannins in the leaves combine with the eau de vie to give the creamy cheese a kick. The cheese is ideally eaten when 2 months old.

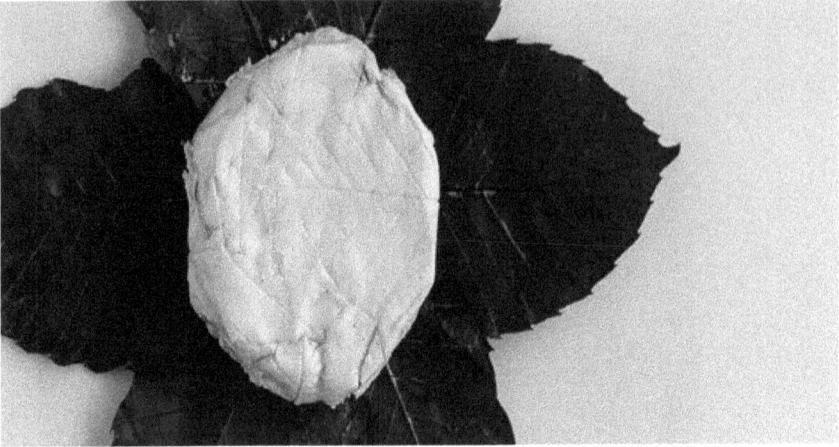

O'Banon cheese wrapped with chestnut leaves

In France, the cheeses go under the name of Capriole Cheese. The O'Banon name is only used in the USA where it is named after one of the Governors of Indiana.

The Healthy Leaf

In recent years, scientists have increasingly focused on traditional herbal remedies and local folklore, particularly as microbial drug resistance becomes a growing concern. Many of these remedies are now being carefully studied to uncover specific compounds with therapeutic potential.

Researchers at Emory University, Atlanta, Georgia, USA, conducted a study on the European or sweet chestnut tree *(Castanea sativa)*, discovering that its leaf extracts contain compounds that neutralize harmful strains of *Staphylococcus aureus*. These extracts are rich in ursene and oleanene derivatives, which are *pentacyclic triterpenes* capable of reducing microbial virulence without encouraging resistance.

The Mediterranean region, with its long and diverse medical traditions, has been a source of inspiration for this research. Many of these traditions persist in the folk medicine practices of local communities. Investigating botanical remedies used for treating skin and soft tissue infections led to the study of chestnut leaf extracts, which show promise as an effective treatment for *Staphylococcus aureus*.

The Mediterranean has a rich history of medical traditions that have developed under the influence of diverse cultures over millennia. Today, many traditions are still alive in the folk medical practices of local people. Investigation of botanical folk medicines used in the treatment of skin and soft tissue infections led to a study of chestnut leaf extracts. Chestnut leaf extract is rich in oleanene and ursene derivatives *(pentacyclic triterpenes)*, that are useful against all *Staphylococcus aureus*.

Chestnut Tea

Sweet chestnut leaf decoctions have long been used in folk medicine to treat various respiratory conditions, including asthma, coughs, colds, bronchitis, and other bronchial issues. The leaves are also known to contain natural antioxidants.

Sweet chestnut leaf tea is prepared by steeping dried leaves in hot water for several minutes. This process creates a unique brew that traditional medicine practitioners often believe provides numerous health benefits

By now you have probably realized that sweet chestnut has many uses, you can even smoke the leaves, dried chestnut leaves can be made into tobacco as these two pictures from Denmark reveal.

Folklore and Sweet Chestnuts

A tree that has been around for so long is bound to attract folklore.

In Corsica, one of the traditional homes of sweet chestnuts, there is a wedding tradition where 22 different chestnut dishes are provided at the wedding.

Whilst travelling through Corsica, John and Linda were told how the villagers kept themselves alive during the Second World War. The invading armies from the north came through the farms and killed off the livestock to try and starve the farmers. Being from north of the

Alps the soldiers were unfamiliar with the values of the sweet chestnut and left the trees alone.

The farmers not only survived but maintained a healthy diet by relying on the chestnut as a staple food during the war. The enemy never understood what was happening nor why the farmers were not malnourished.

To early Christians, sweet chestnuts were a symbol of chastity. In Modena, Italy, chestnuts were soaked in wine and then roasted before being served to celebrate St Martin's Day which falls on November 11th. Many European countries celebrate St Martin's Day with a feast. The Goose is often the basis for the meal and chestnuts as an embellishment to the meal.

In the USA, the Cherokee have used the American chestnut tree for thousands of years to create traditional remedies. They made a cough syrup from its leaves, used them to ease heart issues, and occasionally prepared an astringent tea from young sprouts to help heal sores and wounds.

"That Old Chestnut"

Coming from the United Kingdom, John had often heard the phrase "that old chestnut" which referred to a joke that had been heard many times before. Where did the phrase come from?

In 1816, a play called "Broken Sword" by the playwright William Dimond was performed at the Royal Covent Garden Theatre in London. Part of the script by one of the actors playing Zavior said:

> "I entered the wood at Collares, when suddenly from the thick boughs of a cork tree."

Pablo: (Jumping up says.) "A chesnut, Captain, a chesnut... Captain, this is the twenty-seventh time I have heard you relate this story, and you invariably said, a chesnut, till now."

The play was a success and later played at theatres in the United States of America.

Also in the 1880s, many American newspapers began using "chestnut" to refer to hoary, oft-repeated stories, and the term became established in the common lingo thereafter. The "old" was added later.

Freshly harvested chestnuts at Chestnut Brae

The Chestnut...The Health Nut

Chestnuts are full of natural goodness. Chestnuts, unlike other nuts, are rich in vitamins and minerals and are low in total fat and saturated fat, consisting of only a gram of fat and less than 70 calories in 70 grams. Chestnuts are the only nut which contains Vitamin C, with 85 grams of chestnuts providing your necessary daily intake.

Chestnuts are also rich in folates, supplying the body with B1, B2, B3 and B6 vitamins and folic acid. Folic acid is required to produce red blood cells and DNA synthesis. Chestnuts are a rich source of iron, calcium, magnesium, manganese, phosphorous and zinc, plus a very good amount of potassium. Packed with nutrients, and with slow-digesting carbohydrates makes chestnuts an ideal food to eat while exercising.

Furthermore, chestnuts are also a great source of fibre, which helps lower blood cholesterol levels.

The Health Benefits of Chestnuts

Posted by Hunimed Web Team, 17 October 2016

> "Chestnuts are also excellent sources of vitamins and minerals (such as manganese, molybdenum, copper and magnesium).

What are the nutritional value and the health benefits of chestnuts?

- Digestive health – chestnuts reduce cholesterol levels and stabilise blood sugar levels. They also reduce the risk of constipation and intestinal complications such as diverticulosis.
- Increased brain function – chestnuts contain fat-soluble B vitamins that promote healthy skin, produce red blood cells and improve brain function.
- Increased energy levels – chestnuts contain high amounts of carbohydrates, which are needed for short- and long-term energy. They also help with nervous system function.

- Stronger bones – chestnuts contain copper, which is a trace mineral that enhances bone strength and boosts the immune system.
- Decreased risk of developing disease – chestnuts contain manganese, which is a trace mineral that fights off free radicals in the body and reduces the risk of heart disease and cancer. It also plays a key role in the ageing process and helps prevent blood clotting.
- Do not contain gluten – chestnuts are of great benefit to patients with coeliac disease, which is a disease that upsets the small intestine.

Some nutritional facts about chestnuts- Sabrina Oggionni, Dietitian at Humanitas Gavazzeni, provides some insight on the health benefits of chestnuts and individuals for whom consumption is recommended.

"Chestnuts are a part of the fruit group and some individuals classify them as dried fruit. However, in comparison to nuts (walnuts, hazelnuts, almonds, etc.), they have a low-fat content. Chestnuts have certain nutritional characteristics similar to those of cereals. Even though they do not contain gluten, they do have a high content of sugars, especially starch. Chestnuts are rich in fibre, as well as mineral salts such as potassium, phosphorus, and small quantities of iron. Lastly, they contain vitamins B2 and E. It is important to remember that the energy and nutritional characteristics of chestnuts are different from that of the remaining group of fresh fruits."

https://www.hunimed.eu/news/health-benefits-chestnuts/

Chestnuts ...the Healthy Asian

Chinese folklore often mentions the benefits of chestnuts. Chestnuts have been known to "tonify qi, strengthen the stomach and nourish kidney qi" (from Supplementary Records of Famous Physicians in China). These nuts are lower in calories and fats compared to other nuts and rich in fibres, and fat-soluble vitamins (Ascorbic acid, B1, B2, B3, B6, and E). This makes it super beneficial for lowering blood cholesterol and forming healthy bones and vessels.

Chestnuts are great for people with frequent nausea and loose stools due to spleen and stomach deficiency. It can tonify kidney qi to strengthen bones and the lower back for people suffering from lower back and knee weaknesses. Chestnuts are often labelled as "the fruit of the kidney" in Chinese medicine.

Sweet Chestnut ...the multipurpose tree

At Chestnut Brae, we believe in a no-waste philosophy and feel we should use all aspects of this versatile tree. The small nuts that are discarded by most growers at Chestnut Brae are fed to free-roaming heritage pigs. These pigs produce the best pork you will ever eat.

The most famous chestnut-fed pigs come from around the town of Parma, in Italy. Parma is famous for parmesan (parmigiana) cheese and prosciutto.

Two of Chestnut Brae's chestnut fed pigs

Prosciutto di Parma is salt-cured pork made from pigs raised on a combination of whey from Parma's cheese factories and chestnuts plus the grain from the surrounding countryside. Parma prosciutto is the best in the world.

Lardo di Arnad, an Italian delicacy, is also made from chestnut-fed pigs and in Italy, they have a festival for the lard. This lard is the only European-designated lard and comes from the small town of Arnad in the Valle d'Aosta.

Some connoisseurs argue that the best ham in the world comes from Spain, Jambon Iberico de bellota or Iberian ham where the pigs are raised on a diet of acorns and chestnuts.

THE SWEET CHESTNUT | 39

At Chestnut Brae, we raise our pigs with chestnuts and we believe the pork is the best-tasting pork you will experience.

We use the prunings from our chestnut trees to raise Shitake mushrooms. In Italy Porcini mushrooms grow on the root systems of chestnut trees, so at Chestnut Brae we are trialling that too.

At Harris Farm Market in the eastern states of Australia they sell Chestnut and Almond fed Provenir beef. Llandillo Herford Stud feeds their cattle on chestnuts and almonds to produce some of the best-tasting beef you will ever taste.

What other tree can be so versatile in providing a range of top-quality nourishing foods?

The Story of Flour

Chestnuts make the finest flour.

Chestnut Flour is one of the best flours you can taste. For the recipe "Best ever Paleo Chestnut Bread" go to chapter 8 - Deserts.

The home of chestnut flour is Italy, although there are a few producers globally, including Chestnut Brae in Australia.

On our visit to Corsica, we observed flour being made in ovens. Dried chestnuts are peeled to leave the kernel and this is then ground to make the flour.

How to make Chestnut Flour

- Score the chestnuts, roast at 200 C (400F) for 25 minutes
- Peel chestnuts and chop roughly
- Return to the oven on a very low heat to dry them out for a few hours.

- Blend in a food mill or high-speed processor
- Using a fine sieve sift out the chestnut lumps from the flour.

Flour can come in many different varieties. The type of flour that is used to bake different items is vital to the finished product's look, taste, texture and nutritional content.

But first the history of flour ....

Stoneground flour

The earliest evidence of stones used to grind food is found in northern Australia, at the Madjedbebe rock shelter in Arnhem Land, dating back around 60,000 years. Grinding stones or grindstones, as they were called, were used by the Aboriginal peoples across the continent and islands, and they were traded in areas where suitable sandstone was not available in abundance. Different stones were adapted for grinding different things and varied according to location.

One important use was for foods, in particular, to grind seeds to make bread, but stones were also adapted for grinding specific types of starchy nuts, ochres for artwork, plant fibres for string, or plants for use in bush medicine, and are still used today.

The Australian grindstones usually comprise a large flat sandstone rock (for its abrasive qualities), used with a top stone, known as a "muller", "pounder", or pestle. The Aboriginal peoples of the present state of Victoria used grinding stones to crush roots, bulbs, tubers and berries, as well as insects, small mammals and reptiles before cooking them.

Neolithic and Upper Paleolithic people used millstones to grind grains, nuts, rhizomes and other vegetable food products for consumption. These implements are often called grinding stones and used either saddle stones or rotary querns turned by hand. Such devices were also used to grind pigments and metal ores prior to smelting.

Millstones were introduced to Britain by the Romans during the 1st century AD and were widely used there from the 3rd century AD onwards. (https://en.wikipedia.org/wiki/Millstone)

Stoneground flour versus roller milled (industrially ground) flour

Stoneground flour differs from industrially ground flour in a variety of ways. Grains are milled gently using the stone ground method, being ground slowly between two stones. Three parts make up a grain - the bran, the germ and the endosperm. The bran provides fibre, protein and vitamins that are vital in maintaining a healthy digestive system. The germ provides B vitamins and fatty acids that are necessary for healthy brain function. The endosperm contains starches, carbohydrates, protein, iron and B vitamins. Stoneground milling, which is done in a cool and gentle way, retains these vitamins and nutrients.

On the opposite end of the spectrum, industrially ground flour is ground using high-speed rollers that heat the grain. In this process, the bran and the germ are taken away, and in doing this, important minerals, fats, fibre and vitamins are also eliminated.

When the steel roller-milled flour was first introduced in the 1900s, people protested the new system due to the great loss in nutritional content of the flour. It lacked the proteins, fats, vitamins and mineral constituents present in the original grain. It also was said to upset our gut health or intestinal flora due to the starchy content overload. In 1920, the first head of the Food and Drug Administration (FDA), Dr. Harvey Wiley who advocated for pure foods and drugs in the United States tried to outlaw refined, bleached white flour because of the processes involved with making it, and the loss of nutrition. (http://www.billsorganics.com.au/)

Stone-Ground White Flour versus Roller-mill Bleached White Flour

Stone-ground white flour and roller-mill bleached white flour exhibit distinct nutritional and compositional differences, reflecting their unique processing methods. Stone-ground flour has an extraction rate of 81%, higher than the 72% for roller-mill bleached flour, meaning it retains more of the whole grain's original components. This flour is also higher in protein (11.20% compared to 10.70%) and fat content (1.20% versus 0.70%), likely because stone-grinding preserves more of the wheat germ and bran. In terms of macronutrient balance, stone-ground flour has a lower carbohydrate content (67% compared to 80% in roller-mill flour), which could appeal to those seeking a flour with a less refined profile.

When it comes to minerals and vitamins, the benefits of stone-ground flour are even more apparent: it contains 50 mg of calcium per 100 g, more than double the 22 mg found in roller-mill bleached flour. Stone-ground flour also provides 4 mg of iron per 100 g, compared to only 1 mg in roller-milled flour. Additionally, stone-ground flour retains essential vitamins, boasting 200 units of vitamin A and 150 units of vitamin B1 per 100 g, while roller-milled bleached flour offers none for vitamin A and only 22 units for vitamin B1. Despite these nutritional differences, both types of flour have a similar caloric value of 370 calories per 100 g. Overall, stone-ground flour's higher nutrient density highlights its value as a more wholesome choice in cooking and baking. (resilience.org, 2015)

Health benefits

Many of the health benefits of stone-ground flour come from the milling process itself. The stones used stay cold, unlike industrial mills that effectively burn some important nutrients in the milling process. Wheat germ contains high levels of vitamin E, which has been suggested as a cure for many diseases. The nutritional value of flour that has been stone ground is high, as digestibility is increased through this process.

Health benefits of eating bread with flour that has been stone ground include lowered cholesterol and blood sugar levels. Studies have shown that by having a diet that has a low Glycaemic Index (low GI), weight loss may be easier, a reduction in body fat may be seen and there is a reduction in risk factors for diabetes and cardiovascular disease, all of which lead to a higher quality of life.

Cold Stone Milled Chestnut Flour

In the past the chestnut was called the "bread tree:" Its fruits were so nutritious that they were able to feed farmers during famines, or the inhabitants of areas where grains were scarce. By virtue of necessity chestnut eaters found an effective strategy to stock up on carbohydrates. Pietro Andrea Mattioli, a great Sienese humanist and botanist who lived in the 16th century, narrates: "In the mountains where little wheat is harvested, chestnuts are dried and ground into flour which is skillfully used for making bread."

So, what today is considered a trendy product – used to make pancake dough softer or to enrich vegetable soups with added flavour – a few centuries ago was the only source of sustenance available to destitute families. This explains why **chestnut flour** has inspired numerous recipes and is preserved in the cooking manuals that have made the history of Italian gastronomy.

Chestnut flour: characteristics and curiosities

Chestnut Brae's chestnut flour is prepared by finely cold stone grinding the product after having dried the chestnuts to 4% moisture content. The colour of chestnut flour ranges from light hazelnut to ivory, and compared to chickpea and almond flour, it has a more decisive, slightly sweet flavour. In the kitchen, this ingredient, rich in starch, gives dough a compact and dry texture, which is why it's always necessary to add a sufficient quantity of water to dilute the mixture before baking.

Chestnut flour: properties and nutritional values

Do you know that nutritionists suggest using chestnut flour as a substitute for bread or potatoes? In fact, its nutritional values are characterised by high levels of carbohydrates (75-80%) and by a low quantity of fats (3-4%), with proteins of around 6%.

Chestnut flour is a real concentrate of fibres, capable of slowing down the body's absorption of sugars and inducing a prolonged sense of satiety.

The absence of gluten is another advantage which makes it an ideal food to supplement the diet of people suffering from coeliac disease. Chestnut Flour also has high levels of potassium.

This gluten-free flour can be used to make cakes, crêpes, pancakes, mousse, muffins, cookies, and pastries. It functions delectably in soups and sauces that you can serve alongside chicken, turkey, or game. It must be sifted and combined with bread flour in order to be used in leavening dough to make bread or other baked goods.

From chestnut flour to Castagnaccio... Recipe and pairings.

Born in Tuscany and "adopted" by numerous other Italian regions such as Lazio, Umbria and Emilia-Romagna, Castagnaccio is one of the most popular dishes made with chestnut flour. Despite being a typically autumn dish, in Italy, this thin and dense cake is prepared by village residents throughout the year, including summer. The original recipe features chestnut flour along with water, olive oil, rosemary needles, pine nuts and raisins (with the occasional addition of orange peel and fennel seeds). The "cake" contains no sugar: it is the flour itself that gives the dough sweetness, simple and genuine. The perfect pairing? Try it with Chestnut Brae's Chestnut Liqueur, which is a soft and fruity wine. Garnish your square of Castagnaccio with a dollop of ricotta or mascarpone sweetened with a drizzle of honey and a sprinkle of cacao powder.

Other traditional recipes that employ chestnut flour

Also, in Tuscany you will find **necci**, fragrant crepes made from an amalgam of chestnut flour, water and confectioners' sugar––usually baked in cast iron pans and traditionally stuffed with whipped ricotta––and **manafregoli**: a peasant dish from the area of Garfagnana, made by simmering cow's milk with chestnut flour over low heat until a thick and nourishing cream forms. Among other worthy of mention regional dishes are **taiette** from Lunigiana which are tagliatelle kneaded from a mix of chestnut flour and "0" flour; **gnocchi with chestnut flour from Valchiavenna**, dressed with mushrooms and mountain cheese; sweet **chestnut ravioli** from Piceno, kneaded and fried during the Marche region's Carnevale parades; sweet flour **flan** with chocolate, candied citron and almonds from Barga (a town in the province of Lucca), carefully described in Artusi's *Science in the Kitchen*.

Chestnut flour: other culinary uses

How can we use chestnut flour to prepare something different from classic regional dishes? If you're planning a quick lunch, we recommend making **crepes**: just mix the same amount of chestnut flour and water with a whisk and cook the mixture over low heat in a pan greased with olive oil, flipping it over when the surface starts to ripple.

To test your skills, instead, you can attempt making **bread**, like typical Marocca di Casola. There are many recipes for this, from a gluten-free version with a mix of chestnut flour and rice flour, to one that involves the addition of semolina durum wheat. Choose one according to your tastes and, if you want to go crazy, use a sourdough starter culture.

For Sunday lunch there's nothing better than **fresh egg pasta**, softened by the sweet taste of toasted chestnuts (have you ever cooked chestnut tortelli?). Or a creamy soup made with flour thickened in the broth, rosemary, smoked pancetta and croutons. Any ideas for dessert? You will have a hard time choosing from a chestnut and persimmon cream to cake with chestnut flour and dark chocolate, up to the Aosta Valley chestnut biscuits, there is something for everyone.

However, we suggest you try *bardinsecco*, a very special Tuscan biscuit: below is the recipe of master **Paolo Sacchetti** of the **Nuovo Mondo** pastry shop in Prato.

Bardinsecco recipe by Paolo Sacchetti

Ingredients

- 100 g extra virgin olive oil
- 100 g confectioners' sugar
- 100 g chestnut flour
- 100 g egg whites
- 100 g raisins
- 100 g pine nuts

Instructions

1. Pour the dry ingredients in a stand mixer with the leaf attachment or in a bowl and start mixing them (alternatively, use a spatula).
2. Add the olive oil and egg whites previously beaten to stiff peaks in another container.
3. When the mixture is homogeneously mixed, add the pine nuts and raisins. Spread the mixture as finely as possible on parchment paper or a silicone mat, then bake in the oven at 175-180°C for 8-10 minutes (until the biscuit turns hazelnut-coloured).
4. Cut while still hot into equal sized squares. Once cool, store in a glass jar.

Recipe by Lucia Facchini

Parts of this Cold Stone Milled Chestnut Flour text were taken from https://www.gamberorossointernational.com/news/food-news/chestnut-flour-properties-nutritional-values-and-recipes/

A picker collecting chestnuts at Chestnut Brae orchard

Autumn is Harvest Time

In early autumn, a sweet chestnut orchard is a hive of activity. Chestnuts begin to slowly fall from their burrs in the trees and then within a couple of weeks it begins to rain chestnuts.

With five varieties at Chestnut Brae, we plan on 10 weeks to harvest, although there have been years when we have achieved a harvest in less than four weeks. We endeavour to get the nuts picked and into cool store within 24 hours of the nuts falling to the ground.

The nut has a "burr" which goes brown when the nut is mature inside. At this stage, most fall to the ground, some nuts come clear of the prickly burr whilst others have to be prised out, it depends on the variety of the nut.

Not all the nuts on a tree ripen at the same time and therefore a tree must be visited a number of times at harvest time.

In Corsica, we have seen growers place a net on the ground, let the nuts land on the net and then they scoop the nuts up and grade them.

We have a purpose-built tractor pulled "vacuum" harvester which we rarely use. It clears up the nuts in the orchard exceptionally well, but it collects everything, all the twigs and leaves too, and then that slows the grading up considerably and makes the total job for us much more time consuming.

We also have a purpose-built chestnut harvesting machine, that comes from Italy. It sweeps the nuts into the central area where a large vacuum sucks up the nuts. There is a blower in the machine that blows out most of the leaves and twigs. This machine means that where we in the past used 15 pickers to pick our chestnuts, the machine can be operated by one person.

In the past when we used hand pickers to harvest the chestnuts, it was slow and labour intensive, with the average picker picking around 100kg a day, but it meant the nuts came to the grader beautifully clean and made the grading so much easier for us.

Once harvested, the nuts arrive in the packing shed and are weighed and tipped into a hopper on the grading machine.

We then inspect the nuts on a conveyor belt to ensure the quality standard for market by removing damaged or substandard nuts. The nuts are then graded by size into small, medium, standard, large 1, large 2 and Special.

Once they are graded, they are placed into crates and stored in a cool room at around 1 degree centigrade. They can be stored for around three months before they start to dry off.

Every grower does different things with their nuts.

Our small nuts are fed to heritage pigs for chestnut fed pork, the medium size we peel (pastiglia in Italian) and add value to them and the standard and large sizes go to the fresh market and end up in retail stores. The Specials are that…Special. They are consumed at home. These are the real gems of the trade and are used for Marron Glace in Italy and France.

In the traditional growing areas of Europe nuts are dried to make flour. Go trekking in the mountains of Corsica in Autumn and you will see drying kilns scattered across the countryside. These are in fact smoking sheds. A fire is lit and the chestnuts are layered above the fire for around two weeks. The fires are kept alight during this period and the shed area soon becomes a place to be during this season.

Dried chestnuts have always been part of the staple diet in Italy. During the reign of Napoleon in Italy, chestnuts were so valuable that the governor placed a tax on chestnuts and they were individually counted for tax purposes.

**The peeling
machine at
Chestnut Brae**

At Chestnut Brae, many of our nuts are peeled. We use a chestnut peeling machine that we imported from South Korea. It is based on a potato peeler and saves hours of time trying to peel nuts by hand. We then use the peeled nuts for creating products.

Chestnuts as Fodder

Travel to Europe and you will find pigs wandering the chestnut groves eating the chestnuts, chestnuts make a great food for animals. As the crop ripens on our farm, the kangaroos have a feast.

Cattle Fodder to make the best Steaks.

A newspaper headline in Australia some years back read "Sydney's top restaurants are going nuts over a new steak which comes from chestnut-fed steers."

Top restaurants in New South Wales seek out the rare, sweet chestnut fed steak, which is only available for six weeks of the year. Raised by Michael and Marnie Feneley on 445ha of prime grazing land, the cows are pasture fed but snack on produce from three groves of chestnuts in the autumn months giving the beef a rich aroma and fantastic texture, much like Spain's world famous Jamon Iberico de Recebo, ham from the Iberian pig fed with acorns.

Compared to wagyu, the meat is a bit leaner and the marbling is not as pronounced. *"It's slightly younger beef but the thing I noticed is the texture. It's got this quite buttery, silkiness to it which comes from the oils in the chestnut,"* according to one of the chefs.

In the USA Jackson County (Florida, USA) chestnut producer and the Marianna High School Future Farmers of America (FFA) teamed up in an experiment in the emerging sweet chestnut beef market niche. Chestnuts are added to the diets of the cattle in the last few months of fattening for the market. The nuts give the animals a particularly rich aroma, texture and flavour.

Pig Food to make the best Pork Products

At Chestnut Brae we have become famous for our chestnut fed pork. One of the most asked questions is does it change the flavour of the pork? The answer is a yes, most definitely. Prosciutto from Parma, Italy is famous because the pigs there were first fed on the whey of the cheese made in the area, and then in the autumn, towards slaughtering time, were turned out into the forests to root around for themselves. What they found were lots of chestnuts. Chestnut-finished pork, made from pigs that spend the last few months of their lives on a high-chestnut diet, is well-regarded.

A report by Food Scientist Esther Inglis-Arkell looked at the research. Researchers have looked into the question of why the flavour changes. One study looked at indoor-raised pigs fed commercial feed their whole lives, chestnuts for one month before they were slaughtered, or chestnuts for three months before they were slaughtered. Another study took a look at pigs that were finished on pig feed, mixed pig feed and chestnut, or pure chestnut diets. A third study compared "cured lard" from pigs who were either raised indoors on commercial feed, raised in free range conditions on acorns, or raised in free range conditions on chestnuts.

When it came to pork nutrition, all three studies endorsed the nut-raised pork. Commercial fed pork was consistently higher in saturated fats. Nut-fed meat was higher in monounsaturated fats (often abbreviated MUFA). Chestnut-fed pork had more polyunsaturated fat (PUFA) than acorn-fed or commercial-fed pork. On the other hand, it also had more alpha and gamma tocopherol, which are both vitamin E compounds that are easily absorbed in humans.

So, the research proves chestnut fed pork is the best.

Roasting Chestnuts

> "Chestnuts roasting on an open fire
> Jack Frost nipping at your nose
> Yuletide carols being sung by a choir
> And folks dressed up like Eskimos".

Torme and Wells wrote this song in 1946 and it became a hit the first time around with Nat King Cole. The irony is that the American Chestnut had already disappeared from the culinary scene when the song became popular. Even so, a generation prior hot chestnut vendors could still be seen in many eastern USA cities. This tradition is still strong in Europe with Swiss towns and cities seeming to have the most vendors. In Zurich on a recent trip there seemed to be one on almost every street corner.

Anglo Saxon societies seem to associate sweet chestnuts with roasting.

At farmers markets, when Chestnut Brae cooks hot chestnuts, many customers tell us that it reminds them of their youth and eating hot chestnuts from a charcoal burner "back home."

If you are roasting chestnuts at home heat the oven to 200C/400F/ Gas 6. It is essential you make a cut in the chestnut otherwise it will explode. There are purpose designed chestnut knives, but if you do not have a chestnut knife use a small, sharp knife, cut a cross into the skin of each nut. Place the nuts in a roasting tin and bake them until the skins open and the insides are tender, this takes about 25-30 minutes. If you want to be traditional serve in a paper bag.

The key is to place a cross in the nut before cooking. The reason for this is the nut is 60% water and the buildup of boiling water means the nut will explode if it is not cut. The cut releases the steam.

In Serbia it is traditional to roast chestnuts on Christmas Eve as a treat. Except they do not cut all the nuts. They leave some to explode on purpose. An exploding chestnut heading your way is a sign of good luck.

4

Chestnut - Breakfast

Chestnuts bring natural sweetness and hearty nutrition to breakfast dishes, making them a perfect choice for starting the day with warmth and flavour. These breakfast recipes highlight the versatility of chestnuts, from the crunchy, wholesome blend of Chestnut Granola to the cozy, comforting Chestnut & Apple Spiced Porridge. With options like Keto Breakfast Bars, chestnuts prove to be adaptable for a range of dietary needs, adding fibre, nutrients, and a satisfying richness. Whether enjoyed in a warm bowl or as an on-the-go snack, these breakfasts offer an energising and nourishing start, with chestnuts as the star ingredient.

Chestnut Granola

Chestnuts add a unique flavour and texture to traditional granola (which is toasted muesli), making it a delicious and nutritious snack or breakfast option.

Ingredients:

- 2 cups rolled oats
- 1 cup Chestnut Brae roasted peeled chestnuts, chopped
- 1/2 cup almonds, roughly chopped
- 1/2 cup raisins
- 1/4 cup honey or maple syrup
- 2 tablespoons coconut oil or sunflower oil
- 1 teaspoon vanilla extract
- 1/2 teaspoon ground cinnamon
- Pinch of salt

Instructions

1. Preheat your oven to 165°C (325°F) and line a baking sheet with baking paper or lightly grease it.
2. In a large mixing bowl, combine the rolled oats, chopped chestnuts, almonds, raisins, ground cinnamon, and salt. Mix well to ensure even distribution of the ingredients.
3. In a small saucepan, heat the honey or maple syrup, coconut oil (or sunflower oil), and vanilla extract over low heat. Stir until the mixture is well combined and warmed through.
4. Pour the warm liquid mixture over the dry ingredients in the mixing bowl. Stir well to evenly coat the oats and other ingredients with the sweetener mixture.

5. Spread the granola mixture evenly onto the prepared baking sheet, making sure it's in a single layer.
6. Bake in the preheated oven for about 20-25 minutes, or until the granola turns golden brown, stirring once or twice during baking to prevent burning and ensure even cooking.
7. Once the granola is done baking, remove it from the oven and let it cool completely on the baking sheet. The granola will continue to crisp up as it cools.
8. Once cooled, transfer the chestnut granola to an airtight container for storage. It can be kept at room temperature for up to two weeks.

You can enjoy the chestnut granola as a snack on its own, sprinkle it over yoghurt or add milk, or use it as a topping for desserts. You can add your favourite nuts, seeds, or dried fruits.

Author: Linda Stanley

Chestnut & Apple Spiced Porridge

SERVES 1 time 30 MINS

This porridge is rich, comforting and packed with lots of fibre, healthy fats and protein, making it the perfect breakfast to power you through your day.

Recipe adapted from a recipe by HappySkinKitchen

Ingredients

- 100 gram (3.5oz) Chestnut Brae roasted, peeled Chestnuts
- 1 cup of oats
- 1 cup of oat milk
- 2 tablespoon of almond butter
- 1 teaspoon of cinnamon

For the Stewed Apples

- 1 apple sliced in lengthways slices
- 1 teaspoon of cinnamon
- ½ teaspoon of ground ginger
- ½ teaspoon of ground nutmeg
- 1 tablespoon of maple syrup

Toppings

- Chopped pecans
- More maple syrup

Instructions

1. With a fork mash the chestnuts until you have a crumbly kind of flour.
2. To make the stewed apples simply place the sliced apples and all the spices into a pan with a splash of water. Put the lid on and cook them gently on a medium-low heat for about 20 minutes until they are soft but still keep their shape. Add the maple syrup and cook for another minute. Remove the pan from the heat and leave it on one side
3. To make the porridge: place the oats into a pan with the oat milk and cook them on a medium heat for 5 minutes until most of the liquid has been absorbed. Add the almond butter, the crumbled chestnuts and the cinnamon and stir everything together. Cook for another 5 minutes until the porridge is thick and creamy. Add more oat milk if needed.
4. To serve pour the porridge into a bowl and add the stewed apples on top. Sprinkle with some chopped pecans and drizzle with more maple syrup.

Keto breakfast bars

Prep5 mins Cook 25 min Total 30 min Serves12 Cal

Ingredients

- 1/4 cup / 30g pumpkin seeds
- 1/4 cup / 30g sunflower seeds
- 1/4 cup / 30g ground flaxseed
- 1 tablespoon psyllium husks
- 2 tbsp almond butter
- 1 egg white whisked
- 2 tbsp granulated sweetener – xylitol or stevia
- 1/3 cup sugar free dark chocolate chips
- 1 tsp vanilla extract

Instructions

1. Preheat the oven to 180C - 350 F electric. Line a 6x9 inch (23x15cm) baking tray with baking paper.
2. Pulse the nuts and seeds in a food processor until you have some smaller and some larger pieces.
3. Mix all dry ingredients in a bowl, leaving a few chocolate chips to decorate on top. Then add the whisked egg white, vanilla extract and almond butter and stir until combined. Check and adjust sweetener if necessary.
4. Pour the bar mix into the tray and press down firmly to compact the dough. Press the remaining chocolate chips on top.
5. Bake for 20-25 minutes or until lightly browned. Remove from the oven and let cool completely before cutting into 12 bars.

5

Chestnut - Starters

Chestnuts bring a surprising depth and warmth to savory starters, transforming classic dishes into rich, inviting experiences. These recipes celebrate chestnuts as the main ingredient in a range of appetisers that highlight their versatility and distinctive flavour. From the aromatic sweetness of Roasted Chestnuts in Cinnamon Butter to the creamy, nutty blend of Chestnut Hummus Dip, each recipe captures the chestnut's ability to balance and enhance other ingredients. With recipes like Sage and Chestnut Pesto, which brings a rustic twist to traditional pesto, these starters showcase chestnuts as a refined, yet comforting choice, perfect for setting the tone for a memorable meal.

Roasted chestnuts in cinnamon butter

20m prep 25m cook 4 servings

Ingredients

- 600g (about 24) chestnuts
- 30g butter
- 3 tsp brown sugar
- 1/4 tsp ground cinnamon
- Sea salt flakes, to sprinkle

Instructions

1. Preheat oven to 200°C / 400F. Cut a cross on the flat side of each chestnut. Place on a large baking tray and roast for 20 minutes. Wrap in a clean tea towel. When cool enough to handle, but still quite hot, peel the chestnuts.
2. Melt butter in a large frying pan over medium heat. Stir in chestnuts, sugar and cinnamon for 2 minutes or until combined. Transfer to a bowl. Sprinkle with sea salt.

Recipe by Gemma Luongo - Food writer

- https://www.butterandfleur.com

Chestnut Hummus dip

Prep Time 15 mins + chestnut prep time   Makes 3 cups

Ingredients

Chestnut Hummus Dip image courtesy
Chestnuts Australia

- 500g (1lb) cooked and peeled chestnuts, roughly chopped
- 1-2 garlic cloves, roughly chopped
- 1/3 cup lemon juice
- 1/4 cup tahini
- 1 tsp ground cumin
- 1/4 cup olive oil
- 1/2 cup hot water*
- 1/2 tsp salt

Instructions

1. Combine chestnuts, garlic, lemon juice, tahini, cumin, oil, hot water and salt in a food processor. Process until almost smooth.
2. To serve, spoon into a serving bowl, drizzle with a little extra virgin olive oil, sprinkle with pepper and serve with lavosh or grilled flatbread and cucumber slices.

*Add extra hot water for a smoother and thinner consistency.

Recipe courtesy – Chestnuts Australia – Chestnut Brae is a proud member of Chestnuts Australia

Sage and Chestnut Pesto

A seasonal pesto made from roasted chestnuts and sage. It's versatile too! You can mix it into pasta, thin it out for a vinaigrette, serve it as a sauce for veggies or simply spread it on toast.

Prep Time: 10 minutes Cook Time: 30 minutes Total Time: 40 minutes Servings: 1 cup

Ingredients

- 120 g (4oz) chestnuts
- 1-2 cloves of garlic
- 50 g (1.75oz) Grana Padano or Parmesan, finely grated
- 10 g (.35oz) sage, stems on, woody ends removed
- 10 g f(.35oz) fresh oregano, leaves picked off, stems discarded
- Juice from half a lemon
- Pinch of salt
- 100-200 ml (.5-1 cup)extra virgin olive oil

Instructions

Preheat oven to 200C (400F).

1. Gather the chestnuts and make a horizontal cut across the top of the whole nut, and one cut on each side, providing a larger surface area for the skin to split open and make it easier to peel the nuts. Try not to cut the nut itself (though it's not the end of the world if you do).
2. Arrange the nuts on a baking tray in a single layer, cut side up, and roast for 30-35 minutes. You'll know they're ready when they're golden brown and tender, and the skin has pulled away from the cuts you made.

3. Remove the chestnuts from the oven, wrap them up in a towel and set aside for 5-10 minutes to steam and cool.

4. When cool enough to handle – but still quite hot – peel the chestnuts of both the outer and inner skin layers. The cooler chestnuts get, the harder they are to peel.

5. Roughly break up the nuts into smaller pieces and put them in a bowl of a food processor or immersion blender chopping bowl. Add the garlic cloves and Grana Padano and blitz until the chestnuts are a breadcrumb consistency.

6. Add the sage and oregano, lemon juice and salt, and a quarter or so of the oil and pulse again. Little by little, add oil and pulse until it becomes a pesto consistency – less oil for a thicker, chunkier pesto for dips and sauces, more oil for a smoother, thinner pesto for pasta sauces, vinaigrettes and spreads.

Notes

Use Sage and Chestnut Pesto as: a sauce for pasta, a spread for pizza and sandwiches, a flavour bomb for potato soup, a dip for crudités, a topping for roasted veggies.

Storage: Leftover pesto can be stored in an airtight container and refrigerated for 4-5 days. Or freeze it in small ice cube blocks and store in zip lock bag for up to 3 months.

Author: Eff | Food Daydreaming

https://fooddaydreaming.com/sage-and-chestnut-pesto/

A Pumpkin & Chestnut Feast Menu

Chestnuts and pumpkins are two iconic Autumn produce and both can be the protagonists of seriously mouth-watering dishes, especially to Italians.

The following menu was developed by Via Pompilio Nanni 36, 40050 Monte San Pietro, Bologna. Their advice is:

"To start with a festive glass of Pignoletto, the local sparkling wine, we'll nibble on crispy pumpkin dumplings with a heart of melted local sheep or goat cheese. After that, a thin chestnut flour crepe served with soft fresh ricotta cheese and some slices of cured ham from Calabria, which has the perfect hot personality to complement the sweetness of chestnuts. As a main course potato and chestnut flour gnocchi with a mushroom sauce enlivened with a sprinkle of toasted pine nuts and thin sun-dried tomato stripes. A full-bodied Chianti Classico seemed to us here like the perfect pairing. We divert from our chestnut and pumpkin course only for dessert, for which we plan a scrumptious dark chocolate fondant with homemade mixed citrus jam."

6

Chestnut - Sides

Chestnuts add a unique richness and warmth to side dishes, elevating traditional flavors with their subtle sweetness and earthy profile. This chapter explores chestnut-based sides that bring depth and texture to any meal, from the crisp, golden bite of Chestnut Arancini to the vibrant Roast Chestnut, Olive, and Herb Salsa. Each recipe highlights chestnuts' versatility and ability to pair with a wide range of ingredients, whether in the creamy, delicate Chestnut Ricotta and Honey Cream or the sophisticated contrast of flavors in Candied Chestnut, Blue Cheese, and Fennel Salad. These chestnut sides transform simple ingredients into elegant accompaniments, perfect for enriching any table with a touch of seasonal flair.

Recipe and images courtesy Chestnuts Australia. Chestnut Brae is a proud member of Chestnuts Australia

Chestnut Arancini

Ingredients

- 500g (1lb) chestnuts, cooked and peeled (Note: 800g (1.75lb) of fresh chestnuts produces approx 500g once cooked and peeled)
- 1 ½ cups Arborio rice
- 2 tablespoons olive oil
- 1.25L (5.3 cups) vegetable stock
- 1 brown onion
- 3 cloves garlic, crushed
- ½ teaspoon allspice
- 2 cups fine breadcrumbs
- 2 cups sunflower oil

Chestnut Arancini: Image courtesy
Chestnuts Australia

Instructions

1. Heat olive oil in a large, heavy-based saucepan on medium.
2. Chop the onion very finely and add to the oil. Sauté until softened and slightly golden. About 5-7 minutes.
3. Add minced garlic and continue stirring for a further minute until fragrant.
4. Add rice to the saucepan and stir, coating well.
5. Meanwhile, place the stock in another saucepan and bring to a gentle simmer. Once hot, add a ladle-full to the rice mixture and stir. From here it will need to be stirred constantly until done.

6. As each ladle-full is absorbed into the rice, add another and continue stirring until the rice is cooked and has taken on a creamy, risotto-like texture. The amount of stock used to achieve this may vary but ensure all liquid has evaporated and the rice is soft before turning off the heat.

7. Stir in allspice and chopped chestnuts. Season with salt and pepper. Place risotto mixture in a bowl to cool then refrigerate until cooled completely.

8. Remove risotto from fridge. Fill a shallow bowl with breadcrumbs. Take heaped teaspoons of the risotto mixture, roll into balls and then toss in breadcrumbs.

9. In a large frying pan, heat the sunflower oil on medium. It is ready when a piece of bread turns golden in about 30 seconds. Fry each ball for approximately 3-4 minutes on each side. It should look browned on the outside and be warmed through in the middle. Season with a little salt and pepper. Serve with creamy aioli.

Roast Chestnut, olive & herb salsa

Prep Time 20 mins Cooking
Time 15 mins Serves 4 – 6

Ingredients

- 750g (1.6lbs) of fresh chestnuts
- 1 cup mixed fresh herbs – parsley, thyme, rosemary
- 2 cloves garlic
- 8 tbls extra virgin olive oil
- 3 anchovies, chopped
- 1 tbls capers
- Quarter cup olive flesh
- 2 tbls red wine vinegar
- Salt and pepper

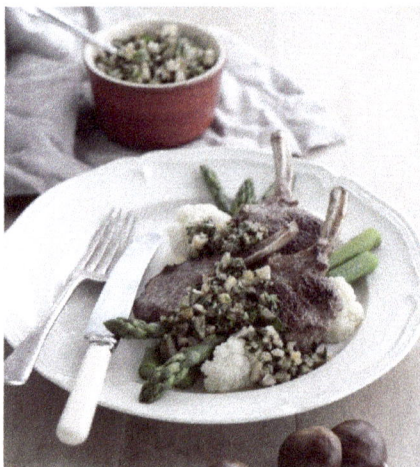

Roast chestnut olive and herb salsa:
Image courtesy Chestnuts Australia

Instructions

1. Score chestnuts and grill.
2. When ready place nuts in a clean tea towel before peeling. Unwrap and peel both the outer shell and the pellicle off.
3. Chop peeled chestnuts to size of large breadcrumbs and mix with remaining ingredients.
4. Season with salt and pepper to taste – perfect for roast or grilled meats.

Chestnuts, ricotta & honey cream

Prep Time 15 mins Cooking
Time 35 mins Serves 6

Ingredients

- 600g (1.3lb) of fresh chestnuts
- 1 tbls honey
- 250g (8oz) fresh ricotta
- 1 tsp vanilla essence
- 150ml pure cream
- 1 tbls caster sugar
- 100g (3.5oz) fresh chestnuts = approx 65g (2.3oz) frozen peeled

Chestnuts, ricotta & honey cream:
Image courtesy Chestnuts Australia

Instructions

1. Score chestnuts and boil till tender.
2. Cut chestnuts and scoop out the flesh.
3. Place in a food processor with honey, vanilla and 2 tablespoons of cold water. Pulse to a smooth paste.
4. Mix chestnut paste with ricotta.
5. In a separate bowl, whip cream with caster sugar to soft peaks.
6. Fold into chestnut ricotta and it's ready to use for pancakes, topping for cakes and accompaniment to fresh or poached fruit.

Chestnut Brussels Sprouts and Pancetta

Prep Time 15 mins Cooking
Time 8 mins Serves 6 – 8

Ingredients

Chestnut Brussels Sprouts and Pancetta:
Image courtesy Chestnuts Australia

- 300g (11oz) of fresh chestnuts
- extra virgin olive oil
- 1 onion
- 2 cloves garlic
- 50g (2oz) pancetta
- 350g (12oz) Brussels sprouts
- 1/4 cup chopped parsley
- Salt and pepper
- 100g (3.5oz) fresh chestnuts = approx 65g (2.3oz) frozen peeled.

Instructions

1. Score chestnuts and place them in a pot of cold water with a couple of pinches of salt.
2. Bring to boil then drain immediately.
3. Allow to cool a little then peel.
4. In a pan heat extra virgin olive oil.
5. Add onion, garlic, pancetta, Brussels sprouts and the chestnuts.
6. Lightly fry for 8 minutes till the Brussels sprouts soften.
7. Add parsley, with salt and pepper and serve.

Easy Roasted Chestnut, Pumpkin and Ricotta Salad

Prep Time 15 mins   Cooking
Time 40 mins   Serves 6 as a
first course

Ingredients

- 300g (11oz) fresh chestnuts (or equivalent
  frozen, peeled fresh)
- 500g (1lb) Queensland
  Blue pumpkin or simi-
  lar
- ½ cup fresh sage leaves
- 3 tbls extra virgin olive oil
- 1 tbls roasted sesame seed
- 150g (5.3oz) fresh ricotta
- Salt and pepper

**Easy Roasted Chestnut, Pumpkin and
Ricotta Salad - image courtesy
Chestnuts Australia**

Instructions

1. Score chestnuts and place in boiling water for 5 minutes till tender.
2. Peel to remove both skin and fine inner pellicle as soon as
   they're cool enough to handle. They'll peel better warm.
3. Peel and deseed pumpkin and cut into 2cm cubes.
4. Place in a baking dish with peeled chestnuts and sage, toss with
   olive oil, salt and pepper.
5. Place in a preheated 180C oven for 30 minutes.
6. Remove from oven and let cool.

7. Slice each chestnut into 5-6 slices.

8. Plate by stacking cubes of pumpkin in a pile on each plate, spoon ricotta around and scatter the sliced chestnuts on top.

9. Use the sage leaves as garnish and any pan juices over the top as dressing.

10. Finish by sprinkling sesame seeds over.

Candied Chestnut, blue cheese & fennel salad

Prep Time 15 mins + chestnut prep time Cooking Time 7 mins Serves 4

Ingredients

Candied chestnuts

Candied Chestnut, blue cheese & fennel salad - image courtesy Chestnuts Australia

- ¼ cup white sugar
- 1 tbls unsalted butter
- 150g (5oz) cooked and peeled chestnuts, quartered

Salad

- 1 bulb fennel, trimmed and halved lengthways (reserve fronds to serve)
- 1 small radicchio, washed and leaves separated
- 150g (5oz) Gorgonzola or similar soft blue cheese, roughly crumbled
- 2 oranges, peeled, all pith removed and sliced into segments
- Extra virgin olive oil, to serve
- Crusty bread

Instructions

To make the candied chestnuts:

1. Heat a non-stick frypan over medium heat.
2. Add sugar and butter and stir until butter melts.
3. Add chestnuts and cook, stirring for 4-5 minutes until chestnuts are golden brown and evenly coated.
4. Transfer to a baking tray lined with baking paper.
5. Separate chestnut pieces and leave to cool.

To make salad:

1. Using a V-slicer or sharp knife, very finely slice fennel.
2. Arrange fennel, radicchio, Gorgonzola and oranges on a serving platter.
3. Sprinkle with candied chestnuts and reserved fennel fronds.
4. Drizzle with extra virgin olive oil, season and serve with crusty bread.

7

Chestnut - Main Course

Chestnuts bring a satisfying heartiness to main dishes, making them an exceptional ingredient in plant-based and savory meals alike. This chapter showcases chestnut-centric mains that offer both richness and nourishment, transforming everyday meals into something memorable. From the robust, slow-simmered flavors of Plant-Based Chestnut Bolognese to the comforting creaminess of Chestnut and Mushroom Risotto, each dish celebrates the chestnut's ability to lend body and depth. Recipes like Chestnut, Wild Rice, and Pecan Stuffed Butternut Pumpkin highlight its versatility, pairing beautifully with other autumnal flavours, while Chestnut Carbonara and Plant-Based Chestnut Dumplings present innovative takes on classic comfort foods. Together, these main courses bring the nutty warmth of chestnuts to the heart of the meal, satisfying both tradition and creativity.

Plant-based Chestnut Bolognese

A plant-based alternative to traditional minced meat spaghetti sauce, made hearty with the rich flavour and texture of chestnuts.

Prep Time 15 mins Cooking Time 90 mins Serves 6

Ingredients

Plant-based Chestnut Bolognese: Recipe and image courtesy Chestnuts Australia

- 500g (1lb) chestnuts, cooked and peeled
- 2 tbsp olive oil
- 1 brown onion
- 3 cloves garlic
- 100g (3.5oz) celery, finely chopped
- 2 medium carrots, grated
- 50g (1.75oz) fresh basil leaves
- 50g (1.75oz) fresh parsley leaves
- 1 tablespoon dried Italian herbs
- 2 tins brown lentils, rinsed and drained
- 200ml (7oz) vegetable stock
- 5 tablespoons tomato paste
- 400g (14oz) crushed tomatoes
- 400ml (14oz) tomato passata (puree)
- 1 teaspoon white sugar

Instructions

1. Heat a large pot with olive oil on medium. Add finely chopped brown onion and sauté for 5 mins, stirring regularly. Add carrot, celery, garlic and dried herbs. Continue sautéing for an additional 10 mins until all vegetables are soft.
2. Coarsely chop chestnuts and add to pot along with finely chopped basil and parsley. Add lentils and vegetable stock. Allow to simmer uncovered for 10 mins.
3. To the pot add crushed tomatoes, tomato passata, tomato paste and sugar. Simmer for approximately one hour. Season to taste and serve with freshly cooked pasta.

Chestnut, Wild Rice and Pecan Stuffed Butternut Pumpkin

Yield: 8 to 9 servings

Ingredients

- 3 1/4 cups (840 ml) water, divided
- 1 cup (240 ml) wild rice
- 1 teaspoon salt
- 2 or 3 butternut pumpkins depending on the size
- Sunflower oil as needed
- 3 stalks celery, finely chopped
- 1 small onion, finely chopped
- 5 cloves garlic, crushed
- 1 tablespoon extra-virgin olive oil
- 400 gm (14oz) cooked peeled chestnuts
- 4 slices wholemeal or sourdough bread
- 250g (8 oz) mushrooms of your choice, chopped
- 2/3 cup (160 ml) coarsely chopped pecans, toasted
- ¾ teaspoon sea salt
- ½ teaspoon dried thyme or 2 tspns fresh thyme, picked
- ½ teaspoon dried oregano or 2 tspns fresh oregano, picked
- ½ teaspoon fresh sage leaves finely chopped
- ½ teaspoon organic rosemary leaves finely chopped
- A pinch of nutmeg
- Freshly ground black pepper
- 1/2 cup chopped parsley

Instructions

1. Preheat the oven to 200C (400F) degrees (Gas Mark 6) and have ready 1 or 2 baking sheets. Combine 3 cups of the water, the wild rice, and salt in a 2-litre (2 quart) saucepan. Cover and bring to a boil over high heat. Reduce the heat to medium-low, and cook for 45 to 55 minutes, or until the rice is tender.

2. Wash the butternut pumpkins, cut them in half with a firm chef's knife, scoop out the seeds, and brush the cavities with the sunflower oil. Arrange the pumpkins on the baking sheet, cut side down, and bake them for 30 minutes.

3. To make the stuffing, combine the celery, onion, remaining 1/4 cup water, garlic, and olive oil in a large, deep skillet. Cook and stir for about 5 to 6 minutes, or until soft and transparent, Transfer to a large bowl along with the chestnuts.

4. Toast the bread until it is dry. Cut it into small cubes and add them to the bowl with the chestnuts.

5. Add the cooked wild rice, mushrooms, pecans, salt, thyme, oregano, sage, rosemary, nutmeg and pepper and mix well. Adjust the seasonings if needed.

6. Remove the butternut pumpkins from the oven and generously fill the cavities with the stuffing. Cover the baking sheets with aluminium foil, shiny side down, and return the pumpkins to the oven for 30 minutes longer, or until tender when pierced with a fork.

7. To serve, cut each stuffed butternut in thirds and sprinkle with chopped parsley.

Recipe adapted from "Vegetarians in Paradise - Chestnut recipes"

Chestnut and Mushroom Risotto

Yield: 6 servings

Ingredients

- 3 large tomatoes, chopped
- 3 to 4 garlic cloves, minced
- 1 medium onion, chopped
- 1/2 cup (120 gm) diced carrots
- 1 stalk celery, diced
- 1 garlic clove, crushed
- 1/4 cup (60 ml) water
- 2 tablespoons extra virgin olive oil
- 700gm mushrooms of your choice, chopped
- 1/2 teaspoon dried thyme or 1 ½ teaspoons fresh thyme leaves, chopped
- 1/2 teaspoon dried sage or 1 ½ teaspoons fresh sage leaves, chopped
- 1/2 teaspoon dried rosemary or 1 ½ teaspoons fresh rosemary leaves, finely chopped
- 1 to 1 ½ cups (300 gm) brown rice
- 1/2 teaspoon lake salt
- 3 to 4 cups (.75 to 1 litre) water, divided
- 400gm Chestnut Brae cooked peeled chestnuts, quartered
- Salt and pepper
- 2 tablespoons fresh minced parsley or chives

Instructions

1. Combine the tomatoes and minced garlic in a large saucepan or skillet. Cook and stir over high heat for about 3 to 4 minutes until the tomatoes have begun to break down. Set them aside to add at the end.

2. Combine the onions, carrots, celery, garlic, water, and olive oil in a large, deep skillet or 8 to 10 litre (10 quart) stockpot. Cook and stir over high heat for 2 to 3 minutes, or until the vegetables begin to soften.

3. Add the mushrooms, thyme, sage, and rosemary and cook for about 2 minutes more, adding as much as a cup (240 ml) of water if needed.

4. Reduce the heat to medium-high and add the brown rice, salt, and 1 cup (240 ml) of the water. Keep the pan simmering and add the water, 1/2 cup (120 l) at a time, as the liquid is absorbed. The process of cooking down and adding water may take 30 to 40 minutes. Taste the rice for tenderness after 30 minutes, it needs to be al dente. You may not need to use all the water.

5. When the rice is tender, add the cooked tomatoes and the chestnuts and cook 3 to 5 minutes longer. Taste and check flavour. It may need another couple of minutes. Season to taste with salt and pepper. To finish, spoon the risotto into shallow bowls and sprinkle with fresh herbs.

Recipe adapted from "Vegetarians in Paradise - Chestnut recipes"

Chestnut Carbonara

Prep Time 10 mins   Cooking
Time 15 Mins   Serves 4

Ingredients

- 500g (1lb) Chestnut Brae cooked peeled chestnuts
- 200g (7oz) chopped nitrate-free streaky bacon
- 250g (.5lb) tubular spaghetti
- 1 tablespoon good quality olive oil
- 3 eggs
- 1 cup grated Parmesan cheese
- 1 tablespoon freshly cracked black pepper

Chestnut Carbonar: Recipe and image
courtesy Chestnuts Australia

Instructions

1. Begin cooking pasta according to packet directions. When it is at the al dente stage, reserve ¼ cup of the pasta cooking water and set aside. Drain pasta and return to pot, adding olive oil.
2. Sauté bacon in a frying pan on medium heat until crispy – about five minutes. Add chestnuts to the bacon and continue stirring over medium heat.

3. In a separate bowl, combine eggs, Parmesan cheese and a generous pinch of cracked pepper.

4. Add the egg mixture to the cooked pasta and stir. Add cooking water and stir before returning to the stove on medium heat.

5. Add half the chestnut bacon mixture and stir to combine. Continue stirring gently until the sauce has thickened and the pasta is warmed through.

6. Serve pasta on plates, topped with reserved bacon and chestnuts. Sprinkle with more cracked pepper and additional grated Parmesan.

7. Serve immediately.

Recipe and image courtesy Chestnuts Australia. Chestnut Brae is a proud member of Chestnuts Australia

Plant-Based Chestnut Dumplings

Prep Time 35 mins   Cooking Time 25 mins   Serves 6

Ingredients

- 500g (1lb) chestnuts, **cooked and peeled***
- 2cm piece ginger
- 2 cloves garlic
- 1 teaspoon sesame oil
- 1 tablespoon oyster sauce
- 3 shallots, finely chopped (reserve some for garnish)
- 1 teaspoon cornflour
- 1/2 teaspoon Chinese five-spice powder

Chestnut Dumplings: Recipe and image courtesy Chestnuts Australia

- 1 275g (10oz) packet round dumpling wrappers (approx 30)
- Soy sauce, chilli oil, black & white sesame seeds, fresh chili and fried shallots for serving

NB: 800g (1.75lb) of fresh chestnuts produces approximately 500g (1lb) once cooked and peeled.

Instructions

1. Place chestnuts, ginger, garlic, oyster sauce and sesame oil into a food processor. Pulse for two minutes or until the mixture starts coming together.
2. Add the shallots, cornflour and Chinese five-spice powder. Stir.
3. Lay dumpling wrappers on a board, eight at a time. Using a pastry brush dipped in water, lightly brush the edges of each wrapper.
4. Place a heaped teaspoon of the filling onto each wrapper and fold it in half using your fingers to seal the damp edges.
5. Bring the two corners of the dumpling together and press to complete the dumpling.
6. Meanwhile, prepare a bamboo or stainless steel steamer by lining it with baking paper that has several holes cut into it for the steam to pass through. Place steamer over boiling water.
7. Steam the first batch of dumplings for ten minutes, while preparing the next.
8. Continue until all dumplings have been made and steamed.
9. Serve with soy sauce, black & white sesame seeds, fresh chilli, chilli oil and fried shallots. Use reserved shallots as garnish.

Roast Pork Loin with Chestnuts, Pistachio and Apricot Stuffing

We discovered this recipe in the Dec 2016 edition of *"Australian Nut Grower "*and it appealed to us as it uses both our passions of pork and sweet chestnuts.

This GF Recipe serves 6 people

Ingredients

- ½ cup whole sweet chestnuts
- 1/3 cup pistachios
- ½ cup roughly chopped dried apricots
- A few fresh chopped sage leaves
- 1.25kg (2.75lb) rolled pork loin, fat trimmed
- 6 cups of steamed vegetables
- 2 large, sweet potatoes, cut into pieces

Instructions

1. Preheat the oven to 200 degrees C (400F)
2. Cut a cross on each chestnut then boil the chestnuts for 15 minutes and remove the outer skin
3. Set aside to cool slightly, then roughly chop
4. Combine chestnuts, pistachios, sage and dried apricots
5. Trim the pork of fat and lay the loin flat
6. Spoon the chestnut, pistachio, sage and apricot mixture over the centre of the pork loin, then roll up and tie with string to secure.

7. Line a baking tray with non-stick baking paper, then place the rolled pork loin on the baking tray. Roast for 1 hour 15 minutes and then rest for 10 minutes.
8. While the roast pork is cooking steam the vegetables and roast the sweet potatoes.
9. Serve with steamed vegetables and roasted sweet potatoes.

Roasted Pork Loin with Chestnuts and Veg

Prep Time 20 mins   Cooking Time 30 mins   Serves 4

Ingredients

Roast Pork Loin with Chestnuts and Veg: Recipe and image courtesy Chestnuts Australia

- 1.2 kg (2.5lb) rolled boneless pork loin, skin on
- 2 teaspoons vegetable oil
- 1-2 teaspoons table salt
- 300g (.5lb) pumpkin, peeled
- 4 medium potatoes, peeled
- 4 small- medium purple onions, peeled
- 1 litre (4 cups) liquid chicken stock
- 2 tablespoons white wine
- 300g (.5lb) green beans, topped and tailed
- 12 Chestnut Brae roasted peeled chestnuts

Instructions

1. Heat the oven to 200°C (400F)
2. Place the pork into a medium roasting tray. Rub with the vegetable oil and
3. Sprinkle generously with salt. Place into the oven for 30 minutes.
4. Chop the pumpkin into 2 – 2.5 cm dice and place into the roasting tray with the pork. Baste with oil from the roasting tray.

Reduce oven temperature to 180°C and place tray back into the oven. Continue to cook for a further 40- 50 minutes, basting regularly until pork is golden and crackling crispy.

5. Place the chicken stock in a small to medium saucepan and bring to a boil. Continue to boil until reduced by half.

6. Remove pork from the oven and rest, covered on a separate plate. Drain fat from the pan, being careful to retain pork juices.

7. Place a baking tray on medium heat on the stove and add the wine, stirring with a wooden spoon to loosen the pan drippings. Add the stock, and boil for 3-5 mins, or until thickened slightly. Add the chestnuts to warm slightly.

8. Bring a small pot of water to the boil. Cook beans for 2 – 3 mins, or until cooked.

9. Meanwhile, slice the pork and serve with the crackling, chestnuts, vegetables and gravy.

Curried Chestnut and Mushroom Pasta

Yield: 4 servings

Ingredients

- 1/2 pound (225g) whole-wheat pasta
- 2 tablespoons extra virgin olive oil
- 1/2 red capsicum/ bell pepper, chopped
- 1/2 cup (160 ml) chopped onions
- 1 clove garlic, minced
- 1 teaspoon salt
- 1/2 to 1 teaspoon curry powder
- 1/2 teaspoon turmeric
- 225gm (1/2 pound) cremini mushrooms, sliced
- 8 shiitake mushrooms, sliced stems discarded
- 2 cups (480 ml) water
- 2 tablespoons corn-starch
- 2 tablespoons water
- 1 tablespoon lemon juice
- 1 cup (240 ml) cooked, peeled, and quartered chestnuts

Instructions

1. Cook the pasta in boiling, salted water according to the manu-facturer's instructions.
2. Heat the olive oil in a large, deep skillet for one minute. Add the capsicum/bell pepper, onions, garlic, salt, curry powder, and turmeric and cook for about 2 minutes.
3. Add the mushrooms and cook another 2 minutes.
4. Add the 2 cups of water and bring to a boil over high heat. Combine the cornstarch and the 2 tablespoons of water in a

small bowl or cup and stir to form a runny paste. Add to the boiling water and stir for 1 minute until thickened.

5. Stir in the lemon juice and chestnuts and mix well. Adjust the seasoning, if needed, and serve overcooked and drained pasta.

A recipe from "Vegetarians in Paradise- Chestnut Recipes"

Chestnut and Capsicum Relish

Yield: 1 1/4 cups (300 ml)

Ingredients

- 2 large red capsicum (red bell peppers)
- 1 cup (240 ml) broken cooked and peeled chestnut pieces
- 1 teaspoon lemon juice
- 1 clove garlic, minced
- 1/4 teaspoon plus 1/8 teaspoon salt
- Pinch of cayenne

Instructions

1. Line a baking sheet with aluminium foil, shiny side down. Place a medium bowl in the sink and fill it with cold water.
2. Put the peppers on the foil and place them under the broiler, 3 inches (7.5 cm) from the heat source. Broil, turning with tongs every few minutes until the peppers are blackened all over. Plunge the peppers into the prepared bowl with water and peel off the skins completely. Discard the core and seeds and transfer the peppers to the food processor.
3. Add the chestnuts, lemon juice, garlic, salt, and cayenne and pulse-chop a few times. Process briefly until all the ingredients are well incorporated but not pureed, allowing the definitive texture of the chestnuts to emerge. Transfer to an attractive bowl and serve immediately or well chilled.

A recipe we discovered in "Vegetarians in Paradise- Chestnut Recipes"

Butternut pumpkin, sage & chestnut rolls

Ingredients

- 1 kg (2lb) butternut pumpkin
- 1 teaspoon dried chilli
- Extra virgin olive oil
- 1 onion, peeled and finely chopped
- 4 cloves of garlic, peeled and finely chopped
- ½ bunch of fresh sage, leaves picked and chopped
- 200 g (7oz) vac-packed Chestnut Brae peeled chestnuts, roughly chopped
- 30 g (1oz) Parmesan cheese, finely grated
- plain flour, for dusting
- 500 g (1lb) all-butter puff pastry
- 1 large free-range egg

Instructions

1. Preheat the oven to 200ºC/ 400ºF /gas 6.
2. Deseed the squash and cut into 8 wedges, then place in a roasting tray and sprinkle over the chilli, drizzle with oil and season. Toss well, spread evenly and roast for 35 to 40 minutes. Remove and cool.
3. Add a drizzle of oil to a pan and place over medium heat. Fry the onions for 10 minutes, until soft, then add the garlic, sage and chestnuts. Continue to fry for 3 to 4 minutes, then add to a large bowl.
4. Remove the skin from the butternut pumpkin and mash the flesh together with the Parmesan and chestnut, onion and herbs, then season.

5. Dust a clean surface with flour and roll your pastry into a 30cm x 45cm rectangle, about 5mm thick and cut into two equal pieces.

6. Beat the egg, then brush the longer side of each piece of pastry with the egg. Place your mashed pumpkin and chestnut filling down the centre, then fold the pastry over, using an egg to seal the edges (press down with a fork).

7. Cut each into 8 equal-sized pieces and place on a lined baking tray.

8. Brush with the egg and bake for 20 to 25 minutes until crisp and golden.

Adapted from a recipe in Jamie Magazine by Jodene Jordan

Chicken and Chestnut Meatballs

Prep Time 25 mins + chilling time + chestnut prep time   Cook time 20 mins   Serves 4

Ingredients

Chicken and Chestnut Meatballs:
Recipe and image courtesy Chestnuts
Australia

- 250g (1.5lb) Chestnut Brae Roasted peeled chestnuts, finely chopped
- 500g (1lb) chicken mince
- 1 small brown onion, finely grated
- 2 garlic cloves, finely chopped
- 1 tsp finely grated lemon zest
- 1 egg, lightly beaten
- 1/3 cup flat-leaf parsley leaves, finely chopped
- ½ cup dry white wine
- ½ cup chicken stock
- 2 tbsp Dijon mustard
- 200ml (7oz) reduced fat sour cream
- 50g (2oz) baby spinach leaves
- Pasta, mashed potatoes or rice, to serve

Instructions

1. To make the meatballs, combine chestnuts, chicken, onion, garlic, lemon zest, egg and parsley in a large bowl. Mix until well combined. Roll mixture into 18 meatballs. Place onto a tray, cover and chill for 20 minutes.
2. Heat oil in a large non-stick frying pan over medium-high heat. Add meatballs and cook, turning often, for 5 minutes until evenly browned. Remove meatballs from the pan and set aside.
3. Add wine to the pan and cook for 1 minute. Stir in stock, mustard and sour cream until well combined. Add meatballs to the pan. Reduce heat to medium-low, cover and simmer, stirring occasionally, for 8-12 minutes until meatballs are cooked through. Toss through spinach.
4. Season to taste. Serve with pasta, mashed potatoes or rice.

Recipe and image courtesy Chestnuts Australia. Adapted by Chestnut Brae a proud member of Chestnuts Australia

Sopa De Castañas (Chestnut and Chorizo Soup)

Serves 4

Sopa de castanas combines chestnut and chorizo for an inviting Spanish soup recipe. Ideal for autumn, the smoky and comforting soup is lovely with crusty bread.

Forests of sweet chestnut thrive in the mountainous regions of Spain. This recipe combines some of the classic flavours of Spanish cooking to produce a warm, comforting and mildly spicy soup that is synonymous with the onset of autumn.

Ingredients

- 4 tbsp olive oil
- 1 large Spanish onion, diced
- 1 medium carrot, diced
- 1 celery stick, thinly sliced
- 120g (4.25oz) mild cooking chorizo, cut into 1cm cubes
- 2 garlic cloves, thinly sliced
- 1 tsp ground cumin
- 1½ tsp finely chopped fresh thyme leaves
- 2 small dried red chillies, crushed
- 2 tomatoes, fresh or tinned, roughly chopped
- 500g (1lb) cooked peeled chestnuts (fresh or vacuum-packed), roughly chopped
- 20 saffron threads, infused in 3-4 tbsp boiling water
- 1 litre (4 cups) water
- Sea salt and black pepper

Instructions

1. In a large saucepan heat the oil over medium heat.
2. Add the onion, carrot, celery, chorizo and a pinch of salt and fry for about 20 minutes, stirring occasionally, until everything caramelises and turns quite brown. This gives the soup a wonderfully rich colour and taste.
3. Now add the garlic, cumin, thyme and chilli and cook for 1 more minute, followed by the tomato and, after about 2 minutes, the chestnuts. Give everything a good stir, then add the saffron-infused liquid, and the water, and simmer for about 10 minutes.
4. Remove from the heat and mash by hand (with a potato masher) until almost smooth but still with a little bit of texture.
5. Season with salt and pepper.

This recipe is by Samuel & Samantha Clark from Moro: The Cookbook

https://thehappyfoodie.co.uk/recipes/sopa-de-castanas-chestnut-and-chorizo-soup/

Spicy chestnut, pumpkin & pancetta soup

This delicious soup thickens on standing, add extra stock if necessary. For extra heat, drizzle soup with sriracha hot chilli sauce.

Prep Time 20 mins + chestnut prep time Cooking Time 40 mins Serves 4

Spicy Chestnut, pumpkin & pancetta soup: Recipe (adapted) and image courtesy Chestnuts Australia

Ingredients

- 1 ½ tbsp olive oil
- 100g (3.5oz) sliced pancetta, chopped
- 1 brown onion, finely chopped
- 2 celery stalks, sliced
- 2 garlic cloves, chopped
- 2 long red chillies, deseeded and chopped
- 500g (1lb) Chestnut Brae peeled and roasted chestnuts
- 750g (1.5lb) peeled and chopped butternut pumpkin
- 5 cups chicken stock
- Reduced fat sour cream and extra sliced long red chili, to serve

Instructions

1. Heat 2 tsp oil in a large saucepan over medium-high heat. Add pancetta and cook, stirring often, for 3 minutes or until crispy. Transfer to a plate. Set aside.
2. Heat the remaining 1 tbsp oil in the pan over medium heat. Add onion, celery, garlic and chillies and cook, stirring often, for 4-5 minutes until softened.
3. Add chestnuts and pumpkin and cook, stirring occasionally, for 5 minutes. Stir in stock and three-quarters of the pancetta. Cover and bring to the boil. Reduce heat, cover and simmer, stirring occasionally, for 20-25 minutes or until pumpkin and chestnuts are tender.
4. Puree soup with a stick blender until smooth. Season to taste. Cover and bring to the boil over medium heat. Ladle soup into serving bowls. Top each with a dollop of sour cream, the remaining pancetta and extra sliced red chilli and serve.

Chestnut, Chicken and Pork Lettuce Cups

Prep Time 20 mins   Cooking
Time 35 mins Serves 8 as a
first course

Ingredients

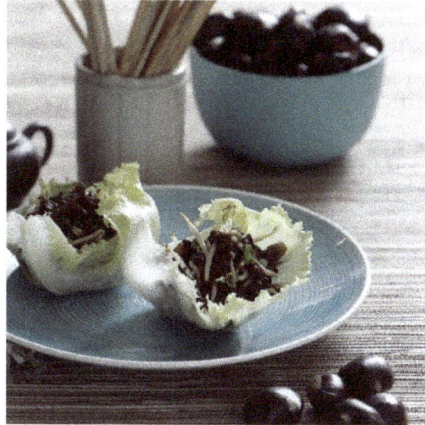

Chestnut, Chicken and Pork Lettuce
Cups: Recipe (adapted) and image
courtesy Chestnuts Australia

- 200g (7oz) fresh chest-
  nuts (or 150g / 5.3oz
  Chestnut Brae frozen
  peeled chestnuts)
- 4 dried Chinese mush-
  rooms (shiitake mush-
  rooms)
- 2 tbls extra virgin olive
  oil (or peanut oil)
- 2 garlic cloves, minced
- 2 tbls finely grated fresh ginger
- 200g (7oz) chicken mince
- 200g (7oz) pork mince
- 4 green shallots, ends trimmed, finely sliced
- 1 tbls Shaoxing wine (or dry sherry)
- 1 tbls oyster sauce
- 1 tbls dark soy sauce
- 1 cup bean sprouts
- 1 tsp sesame oil
- Pinch of salt
- 8 iceberg lettuce leaves, washed, dried and trimmed

Instructions

1. Score chestnuts by cutting a shallow cross on the flat side with the tip of a sharp knife and place in boiling water for 5 minutes. Peel as soon as they're cool enough to handle. Just peel the outer skin and leave the fine pellicle on. Chop chestnuts into ½ centimetre pieces.

2. Place dried mushrooms in a bowl of hot water and soak for 30 minutes. Drain, remove and discard the tough stem, chop each mushroom into ½ centimetre dice and keep aside.

3. Heat the oil in a wok or large frying pan over medium-high heat. Add chopped chestnuts, garlic and ginger and stir for a minute. Add the mince. Stir-fry with a spoon to break up any lumps for 3-4 minutes until the mince changes colour. Add the shallots and stir through. Add wine, oyster and soy sauces and stir through for a minute. Add bean sprouts and sesame oil, stir through and remove from heat. Check for seasoning and add a little salt if necessary. Spoon mixture into lettuce cups and serve.

8

Chestnut - Desserts

Chestnuts lend their naturally sweet, nutty flavour and smooth texture to a range of desserts, making each bite both comforting and indulgent. This chapter is a celebration of chestnut-based sweets that blend classic and innovative flavours, perfect for any occasion. Each recipe highlights the chestnut's unique ability to enhance and balance flavours. Treats like Maple Chestnut Apple Strudel and Maple Roasted Chestnuts bring a rustic richness, while Chestnut Pastry Swirls add an elegant, flaky touch. These desserts offer a delightful way to enjoy chestnuts' versatility and create memorable endings to any meal.

Creamy Chestnut Tiramisu

Prep Time 20 mins   Cooking Time 35 mins   Serves 10 – 12

Ingredients

Chestnut Tiramisu: Recipe and image courtesy Chestnuts Australia

- 500g (1 lb) fresh chestnuts (or 350g / 12 oz Chestnut Brae frozen peeled)
- 250ml (1 cup) milk
- 3 tbls brown sugar
- 1 tsp vanilla essence
- 3 eggs, separated
- 100g (3.5 oz) caster sugar
- 300g (11 oz) mascarpone
- 32 Savoiardi biscuits (Italian sponge fingers)
- 400ml (1.7 cups) water
- 4 tbls cocoa powder plus 1 tsp for dusting

Instructions

1. Score chestnuts and place in boiling water for 10 minutes. Peel to remove both skin and fine inner pellicle as soon as they're cool enough to handle. They'll peel better warm.
2. Thinly slice 8 peeled chestnuts. Place the rest in a small pot with milk, brown sugar and vanilla essence. Simmer on very low heat for 15 minutes until chestnuts become very soft. Remove from heat and set aside to cool, then blend in a food processor

until smooth. If necessary, add 3-4 tablespoons more milk to get a creamy consistency.

3. Beat egg yolks and caster sugar together until the mixture becomes pale. Beat the whites in a separate bowl until they form fluffy peaks.

4. Mix the yolk and sugar mixture together with the mascarpone, then fold the whites in gradually.

5. Mix 4 tablespoons of cocoa powder with 100ml of water to dissolve, then add the remaining water.

6. Dip 8 biscuits two at a time for a second on each side in chocolate water, then arrange in a layer on the bottom of a high-sided 26cm serving dish.

7. Spread on a layer of the mascarpone and then dollop on some chestnut puree, spreading with a spatula. Repeat the process until all the biscuits and mascarpone have been used up, finishing with a layer of mascarpone on top. Scatter the sliced chestnuts over and sprinkle with remaining cocoa powder.

Chestnut, Pear and Orange Powerballs

Prep Time 15 mins   Cooking Time 60 mins   Makes 36 balls

Chestnut, Pear and Orange Powerballs:

Recipe and image courtesy Chestnuts

Australia

Ingredients

- 500g (1lb) fresh chestnuts
- 1 tbs honey
- 2 tbls vegetable oil
- Juice of 1 orange
- 100g (3.5 oz) dried pear, roughly chopped
- 1 tsp ground cinnamon
- ¼ tsp sea salt
- 1 tbls white sesame seeds
- Additional black and white sesame seeds to coat

Instructions

1. Place chestnuts in a medium saucepan with about 1 litre (4 cups) of water, so the chestnuts are fully submerged. Bring to the boil, and boil for 1 hour, topping up water if required. Drain and cool in cold water. When cool enough to handle, open and scoop each nut out.
2. Place chestnut in a mortar and pestle or food processor, and grind until smooth.
3. Add remaining ingredients and process until well combined.
4. Roll tablespoons of the mixture into balls, and coat with a combination of black and white sesame seeds.

Chestnut Paste

by *Chef Eddy Van Damme*, December 15, 2009

1. Chestnuts are absolutely delicious when roasted, candied or puréed into a paste. Chestnut paste can be used in countless ways and is easily prepared at home or in a professional setting. In well-stocked markets, canned chestnut paste is available but oftentimes tends to be overly sweet, making it useless for many preparations. Therefore, make your own chestnut paste.

2. The chestnut paste is delicious on gelato, sandwiched between thin cookies or used in chocolates as a filling. The paste looks amazing when passed through a garlic press, gently shaped into a sphere and placed on a tempered chocolate square. If you do not like to fuss with making your own chocolate squares, you can purchase premade chocolate cups.

3. Getting it all together! Purchase even-sized chestnuts with shiny dark skins. I like to get at least about 2 lb 8 oz. (1140g). Smaller amounts always make it harder to get the chestnuts pureed smoothly in a food processor. Any extra chestnut paste can be easily frozen and used later. When peeling the chestnuts, it helps to have latex or vinyl gloves to protect your hands from the freshly boiled chestnuts.

4. Cold chestnut puree is delicious and makes beautiful petit fours. The paste can be used as it is or mixed with a small amount of buttercream. If desired the paste can slightly be conditioned using simple syrup. A small amount of chestnut liqueur can be added. Press the paste through a garlic press and shape it onto a chocolate square or Gerbet macaroon. Decorate as desired.

Chestnut Paste

6 Cups	(2 lb 8 oz)	Chestnuts -1140 g
2 Cups	(1 lb)	Extra fine granulated sugar - 480 g
1 Cup	(8 oz)	Water -240 g
2 teaspoons	(2 tsp)	Vanilla bean paste or vanilla - 10 g

1. Using a knife, cut a X into the flat side of the chestnuts. It is best to boil the chestnuts in smaller batches as they will peel much better when removed fresh out of hot water.
2. Place part of the chestnuts in a non-reactive pot and cover the nuts completely in water. Bring to a boil
3. Boil for 7-8 minutes and remove using a slotted spoon. Peel away the outer skin and any brown skin on the chestnuts. Repeat until all the nuts are peeled.
4. Place the peeled chestnuts in fresh water and bring to a boil. Reduce the heat to simmer and cook for 15 minutes. The chestnuts should feel "al dente" at this stage.
5. Drain and place the chestnuts in a food processor.
6. Place the sugar in a small saucepan and add 1 cup (8 oz or 240 grams) of water; stir to a boil. Once boiling brush away any sugar crystals stuck to the side of the pan with a clean brush dipped in water. Any additional water added during this process has no effect on the outcome.
7. Cook the sugar syrup WITHOUT stirring to 116°C (240°F).
8. Remove from heat and mix in the chestnut mixture. Stir for 5 minutes on medium heat. Add the vanilla and combine well.
9. Store in a well-sealed container in the refrigerator or freezer.

Recipe from https://chefeddy.com/2009/12/chestnut-paste/

Swiss Vermicelles

Think of Switzerland and sweet chestnuts and you think of a winter's meal with Vermicelles. Vermicelles are made from a sweetened chestnut paste which includes chestnuts, sugar, milk and kirsch.

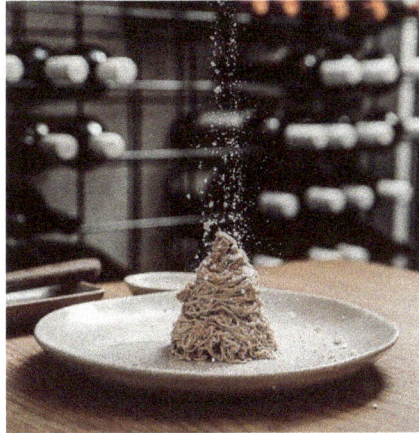

Vermicelles: Image courtesy Balthazar Perth

Vermicelles are prepared in a variety of ways. In Switzerland, you can find them in pastry tarts, in ice cream "coupes", on their own with a dollop of cream or on meringues with sometimes both cream and ice cream.

Once you have made the paste you then need to then push it through a special "Vermicelles press" to create the long strips of spaghetti-like tubes about 15 cm long. You can now create your own desserts with meringue, ice cream or cream.

Homemade Vermicelles Recipe

Ingredients

- 500 – 600g (1-1.3lbs) - chestnuts
- 1 litre milk (4.25 cups) (you can also use water instead for a different texture)
- 2 teaspoons vanilla extract
- 100 g (3.5 oz) caster sugar (you can use slightly less as this makes it quite sweet)
- 1 shot kirsch

Instructions

1. First of all, make an incision in the shell of each chestnut and cook in a pan of boiling water for around 10 minutes.
2. Shell the chestnuts then place them in a saucepan with the milk and sugar and bring to a boil and simmer for 30 minutes until the chestnuts are soft.
3. Add the vanilla, kirsch and a pinch of salt and purée with a stick blender till smooth, adding extra milk if the mixture is too stiff.
4. Allow to cool and then use the Vermicelles press to create the long "worms" of chestnut paste. Sometimes after cooling the mixture becomes a bit more set and needs a drop of milk to loosen it up.
5. Once you have created your Vermicelles spaghetti you can then serve with cream and ice cream or with whipped cream and meringues or put in little pastry cases.

Recipe from https://newinzurich.com/2019/12/vermicelles-a-traditional-chestnut-dessert-from-switzerland/ accessed 2023-12-12

Maple Chestnut Apple Strudel

Yield: about 21 to 24 slices

Ingredients

- 1/2 cup (120 ml) sliced almonds, toasted

Topping

- 2 tablespoons organic sugar
- 1/4 teaspoon ground cinnamon

Filling

- 2 cups (480 g) peeled and roasted Chestnut Brae Chestnuts, coarsely chopped
- 1 cup (240 g) raisins
- 1 cup (240 g) organic sugar
- 1/2 cup (120 g) pastry flour
- 1 1/2 teaspoons ground cinnamon
- 1/4 cup (60 g) maple syrup
- 1 teaspoon organic vanilla extract
- 1 teaspoon maple syrup
- 3 tablespoons lemon juice
- 1 kilo (2 pounds) Granny Smith apples, peeled, cored, cut into eighths and sliced

Dough

- 15 sheets of filo dough, thoroughly defrosted*
- 1/3 cup (80 ml) sunflower oil (approximately)

Instructions

1. Have ready a lightly oiled Swiss roll pan. Place the toasted almonds in a small bowl and set it aside. Combine the organic sugar and cinnamon in another small bowl and set it aside.

2. To make the filling, combine the chestnuts, raisins, organic sugar, flour, and cinnamon in a large bowl, stir well, and set aside. Combine the maple syrup or honey, vanilla and maple syrup in a small bowl, and set it aside.

3. Measure the lemon juice into a separate large bowl and stir in the apples, coating them well to prevent them from turning brown. Set it aside.

4. Preheat the oven to 180C / 350 F degrees (Gas Mark 4) and clear off the kitchen counter. You'll need lots of working room to prepare the filo dough. Place a tea towel vertically on one end of the counter. Open the package of filo and unroll the dough. Place it on the towel and cover the dough with another tea towel to prevent it from drying out. Each time you remove a filo sheet, be sure to re-cover the dough. For convenience, place the sunflower oil in a small bowl.

5. Remove one sheet of filo and lay it on the counter horizontally in front of you. Using a pastry brush, coat the dough lightly with the sunflower oil. Remove a second sheet of filo, lay it over the first sheet, and brush it with oil. Repeat the process until you have 5 sheets altogether.

6. Combine the sliced apples with the toasted almonds, chestnut mixture, and maple syrup mixture and stir well to distribute the ingredients evenly.

7. Place one-third of the filling horizontally along the centre of the filo dough, leaving 1 1/2 inches (3.5 cm) on either end. Lift one horizontal edge and fold it over the filling. Tuck in both of the sides. Then, fold the remaining horizontal edge over and brush lightly with oil.

8. Place the roll on the prepared baking sheet, seam side down, and brush lightly with oil. Repeat the process with two more rolls, placing all three rolls on the baking sheet. Sprinkle the reserved organic sugar and cinnamon mixture over the tops.

9. Use a serrated knife to cut 1 1/2-inch (3.5 cm) slices halfway through. Bake for 45 minutes. Remove and cool for about 10 minutes, then cut through the slices. Use a spatula to transfer them to a large, attractive serving platter. Serve warm, room temperature, or chilled. Refrigerated, leftover Maple Chestnut Apple Strudel will keep for up to 5 days.

Adapted from a recipe in "Vegetarians in Paradise -Chestnut Recipes"

Chestnut Pastry Swirls

Prep Time 25 mins   Cooking Time 1 hr   Makes approx 40

Instructions

1. Remove puff pastry from the freezer and allow to thaw slightly at room temperature.
2. Preheat oven to 180°C (350°F) fan forced.
3. Place cooked chestnuts into a food processor and pulse for about one minute. Add softened cream cheese, cocoa, brown sugar, vanilla and cinnamon. Blitz to form a spreadable paste.
4. Lay the four sheets of puff pastry on the bench and spread the chestnut mixture evenly over each one using a spatula or blunt knife. Roll each square of pastry into a log and slice discs approximately 1.5 cm thick.
5. Place the discs flat onto a lined baking sheet. Be careful not to overcrowd them as they will expand while baking. Brush each one with beaten egg.
6. Bake for approximately 15 minutes or until puff pastry has risen slightly and is golden in colour. Allow to cool slightly before dusting with icing sugar.

Chestnut Pastry Swirls: Recipe and image courtesy Chestnuts Australia

Gluten-free chestnut brownies

Prep Time 20 mins + chestnut prep time Cooking Time 25-30 mins Serves 16 pieces

Ingredients

Standard self-raising flour can be used for a non-gluten-free version.

Gluten-free Chestnut Brownies: Recipe and image courtesy Chestnuts Australia

- 350g (12oz) cooked and peeled chestnuts
- 200g (7oz) good quality 100% dark chocolate, broken into squares
- 200g (7oz) unsalted butter, chopped
- 1 ¼ cups brown sugar
- 1 tsp vanilla extract
- 4 eggs, lightly beaten
- 1/2 cup gluten-free self-raising flour
- 2 tbsp cocoa
- Pinch salt

Instructions

1. Preheat oven to 180°C or 160°C fan forced (350F). Grease and line a 16cm x 26cm x 2-3cm deep slab pan with baking paper, leaving a 2cm overhang on the sides of the pan.
2. Set aside 50g (2oz) of cooked and peeled chestnuts. Place the remaining chestnuts into a food processor. Process until fine

crumbs form (you'll need 2 cups of ground chestnuts). Set aside.

3. Place chocolate and butter in a large microwave-safe bowl and microwave on high for 2 minutes, stirring with a metal spoon every minute until melted. Set aside to cool.

4. Using a metal spoon, stir in sugar, vanilla and eggs into the chocolate mixture until well combined. Sift over flour, cocoa and salt. Stir to combine. Gently fold through chestnuts. Pour into prepared pan. Chop reserved chestnuts and sprinkle over the mixture. Bake for 25-30 minutes until a skewer inserted comes out with moist crumbs sticking. Cool completely in the pan. Cut into squares. Serve with whipped cream and a dusting of cocoa if desired.

Sweet chestnut cream

Prep Time 15 mins   Cooking Time 45 mins   Makes about 2½ cups

Ingredients

- 200g (7oz) cooked and peeled chestnuts
- 450ml (2 cups) pouring cream
- ½ cup milk
- ½ tsp vanilla extract
- 2 tbls caster sugar

Sweet Chestnut Cream: Recipe and image courtesy Chestnuts Australia

Instructions

1. Combine chestnuts, 300ml (1.25 cups) cream, milk, vanilla and sugar in a medium saucepan. Bring to the boil, stirring until sugar dissolves, over medium heat.
2. Reduce heat and simmer (do not boil), stirring occasionally, for 30-35 minutes until chestnuts are very tender. Remove from heat and cool slightly. Using a hand blender, blend until smooth. Transfer to a bowl, cover and chill until cold.
3. Whip the remaining cream in a bowl until soft peaks form. Fold cream through the chestnut mixture and serve.
4. Serving suggestions for sweet chestnut cream:

   ◦ Layer with crumbled Anzac biscuits, diced strawberries and grated chocolate in serving glasses.
   ◦ Use in a filling for sponge cake or butterfly cakes.

- ◦ Spoon over poached pears or quinces.
- ◦ Serve with and fresh sliced pear.

*Store chestnut cream in an airtight container in the fridge for up to 4 days.

Recipe and image courtesy Chestnuts Australia. Chestnut Brae is a proud member of Chestnuts Australia

Chestnut & golden syrup pudding

Prep Time 20 mins + chestnut prep time   Cooking
Time 25 mins   Serves 4 – 6

Ingredients

Chestnut & golden syrup pudding:
Recipe and image courtesy Chestnuts
Australia

- 150g (5oz) Chestnut Brae cooked peeled chestnuts
- 1/2 cup milk
- 1 egg
- 80g (3oz) butter, melted
- 2 tbls golden syrup
- 1/3 cup firmly packed brown sugar
- 1 1/4 cups self-raising flour, sifted
- Icing sugar, for dusting
- Cream or ice-cream, to serve

Sauce

- 1/2 cup brown sugar
- 2 tsp cornflour
- 1 1/4 cups boiling water
- 1/4 cup golden syrup

Instructions

1. Preheat oven to 180°C/160°C fan forced / 350F. Lightly grease an 8-cup (about 6cm deep) ovenproof dish.
2. Finely grate chestnuts in a food processor. In a large bowl, combine milk, egg, butter and golden syrup. Stir in grated chestnuts, sugar and sifted flour. Using a large metal spoon, mix until just combined. Spoon into the prepared dish.
3. To make the sauce, combine sugar and cornflour in a small bowl. Sprinkle over pudding. Combine water and golden syrup in a jug. Pour the mixture over the back of a large metal spoon over the pudding batter. Place the dish on a baking tray lined with baking paper.
4. Bake for 50-55 minutes until golden and the pudding bounces back when gently pressed in the centre. Stand for 5 minutes. Dust with icing sugar. Serve with cream or ice cream.

Recipe and image courtesy Chestnuts Australia. Chestnut Brae is a proud member of Chestnuts Australia

Maple Roasted Chestnuts

Prep Time 15 mins Cooking Time 25 mins Serves 4 – 6

Ingredients

- 500g (1lb) of fresh chestnuts, roasted and peeled
- 150ml (½ cup) maple syrup

Maple Roasted Chestnuts: Recipe and image courtesy Chestnuts Australia

Instructions

1. Turn oven to 180° C (350F)
2. Place the chestnuts and maple syrup into a small roasting tray.
3. Stir to combine, and place into the oven.
4. Stir every few minutes until the maple syrup has thickened and is coating the chestnuts. (About 10- 15 mins).
5. Remove from the oven and allow to cool. Chestnuts should be covered with a sugary- toffee-like coating.

Best ever Paleo Chestnut Bread

Makes 1 loaf Cooking time   40 minutes

Ingredients

Dry ingredients:

- 1 cup (100g) chestnut flour, sieved
- 1/2 cup (65g) extra fine almond flour
- 1/4 cup (28g) coconut flour, sieved
- 1 teaspoon baking soda
- 1/2 teaspoon salt
- 2 tablespoons (25g) sesame seeds
- 2 tablespoons (25g) poppy seeds
- 2 tablespoons (20g) pumpkin seeds

Wet ingredients:

- 5 large eggs (70g each), separated (or 6 medium eggs, 55g each)
- 1/4 cup (60ml) olive oil, plus a little extra for greasing the tin
- 1/4 cup (60 ml) water
- 1 tablespoon apple cider vinegar

Instructions

1. Preheat the oven to 160°C (340°F). Place a small bowl of water on the bottom shelf of the oven (this will steam the loaf and stop the top from cracking). Lightly grease a 900g (2lb) loaf tin with olive oil, and line the bottom with baking paper.
2. Combine the dry ingredients in a bowl (chestnut flour, almond flour, coconut flour, baking soda, salt, sesame seeds, poppy seeds, pumpkin seeds). Mix well with a spatula.

3. Put the egg whites in a clean, dry bowl and whisk with an electric whisk for 1-2 minutes, until soft peaks form. Set aside.

4. In a separate bowl, combine the wet ingredients (egg yolks, olive oil, apple cider vinegar), and mix until blended using an electric whisk.

5. Tip the dry ingredients into the bowl containing the wet ingredients and mix until blended using a spatula. The mixture will be fairly stiff.

6. Lighten the mixture by stirring in half of the whisked egg whites. Tip in the rest of the egg whites and gently fold in using a spatula: cut down the centre with the side edge of the spatula; scrape across the bottom of the bowl and up the side, scooping up the mixture as you go so that it is turned over and under; rotate the bowl 90° and repeat until fully blended. Be careful not to overwork the mixture and knock out the air, but make sure the bitter egg white is fully blended.

7. Scrape the batter into the prepared tin. Smooth the top using a spatula dipped in water. Bake for 40 minutes, or until cooked. When cooked, the top of the loaf should have a brown crust and feel firm to the touch. Do not open the oven door before 40 minutes (this will cause the air in the loaf to collapse).

8. Remove from the oven and leave to cool for about 10 minutes, before popping out of the tin and onto a wire cooling rack. Peel off the baking paper from the bottom.

9. Serve in slices or toasted and spread with marmalade or jam.

10. Store in an airtight container at room temperature for up to 5 days

Recipe from Paleo Pantry accessed 2023-12-12
http://www.paleopantry.org/best-ever-paleo-chestnut-bread/

Chestnut Ice Cream

This is one of our family make chestnut ice cream the family soon tucks in. It can be made in a regular ice cream maker.

Ingredients

- 1/2 vanilla bean
- 2 cups heavy cream
- 1 tablespoon sugar
- 3 tablespoons unsweetened chestnut purée
- 4 large egg yolks

Equipment required

- An instant-read thermometer; an ice cream maker

Instructions

1. Halve vanilla bean lengthwise and scrape seeds using tip of a sharp knife into a 1-1.5 litre (1 1/2- to 2-quart) heavy saucepan. Add pod, cream, sugar, and chestnut purée and bring to a simmer, whisking until chestnut purée is broken up and sugar is dissolved. Remove from heat and cover pan. Let stand 15 minutes.

2. Whisk together yolks in a medium bowl, then add warm cream mixture in a slow, steady stream, whisking constantly. Pour egg mixture back into saucepan and cook over moderately low heat, stirring constantly with a wooden spoon, until custard is thick enough to coat back of spoon and registers 75°C (170°F) on thermometer. Pour custard through a fine-mesh sieve into a clean metal bowl, discarding vanilla pod and forcing chestnut

purée through sieve. Set bowl in a larger bowl of ice and cold water and let stand, stirring occasionally, until cold, 15 to 20 minutes.

3. Freeze custard in ice cream maker until soft-frozen, 20 to 25 minutes, then transfer to an airtight container and put in freezer to harden, about 3 hours.

Chestnut Pudding

This is another of our other family favourites. It is a dessert that is also enjoyed in Quebec where they use Maple syrup with chestnuts.

This recipe is from Maple: 100 Sweet and Savory Recipes Featuring Pure Maple Syrup, by Katie Webster.

Ingredients

To make the Sauce

- 4 tablespoons (55 g) unsalted butter
- ½ vanilla bean, split lengthwise and scraped
- ½ cup (120 ml) maple syrup (preferably dark)
- ¼ cup (60 ml) brewed coffee

To make the Pudding

- ½ cup (50 g) chestnut flour
- ¼ cup (35 g) sweet white rice flour
- ¼ cup (25 g) GF oat flour
- 2 teaspoons (9 g) baking powder
- ½ teaspoon fine sea salt
- 2 large eggs
- ⅓ cup (80 ml) well-shaken, low-fat buttermilk
- ⅓ cup (80 ml) maple syrup (preferably dark)
- 2 tablespoons (30 ml) mild vegetable oil, such as sunflower
- whipped cream, lightly sweetened with a drop of maple syrup and vanilla extract, for serving (optional)

Instructions

1. Position a rack in the centre of the oven and preheat to 350ºF (175ºC). Place 8 (4-ounce) oven-proof ramekins or canning jars on a baking sheet and spray them lightly with cooking oil (or brush with a bit of melted butter).

2. Place the butter and vanilla pod and scrapings in a medium, heavy-bottomed saucepan and cook over medium-low heat, swirling occasionally. After about 3-5 minutes, the butter will foam up, turn golden and smell nutty, with brown flecks mingling with black vanilla bean seeds on the bottom of the pan. At this point, remove the pan from the heat, carefully pour in the maple syrup and coffee, transfer to a measuring pitcher, and set aside.

3. To make the batter, sift together the chestnut, sweet rice and oat flours with the baking powder and salt into a large bowl. Make a well in the flour mixture, and add the eggs, buttermilk, maple syrup and oil. Whisk until well-combined.

4. Pour or scoop the batter into the ramekins, dividing it evenly. Give the sauce a good stir to combine (the butter won't want to emulsify, so you'll want to stir, pour, stir, pour...) and pour it over the batter, dividing it evenly; it will pour through the batter, which is fine.

5. Bake the puddings until puffed and golden, with bubbling sauce beneath the cakey bits, 18-22 minutes. Remove from the oven and let cool at least 15 minutes. Sprinkle with powdered sugar if you like. Serve the puddings warm, passing whipped cream at the table. The puddings are best when freshly baked, but they keep well, refrigerated airtight, for up to 3 days. Reheat in a 350ºF / 175 ºC oven until warm for best results.

9

Chestnut - Drinks

Chestnut drinks are a celebration of warmth, tradition, and the natural sweetness that this ancient nut brings to every cup. From creamy, dairy-free alternatives to chestnut-infused teas, liqueurs, and festive blends, chestnuts have long been used to create unique and nourishing beverages. In this chapter, we explore a variety of recipes that highlight the versatility of chestnuts, including the smooth **Creamy Chestnut Milk**, a wholesome alternative to traditional milk, and the earthy **Castagnaccio Latte**, a classic Italian chestnut milk with a touch of cinnamon. We also delve into the subtle flavors of the Japanese-inspired **Kurigohan Cha**, an infusion of roasted chestnuts, rice, and green tea, as well as the decadent **Crème de Marrons Liqueur**, a sweet chestnut liqueur perfect for special occasions. These recipes capture the rich, velvety texture and subtle sweetness of chestnuts, inviting you to savour their timeless appeal in a variety of drinks that warm the body and spirit.

Creamy Chestnut Milk

Yield: about 1 1/2 cups (360 ml)

Ingredients

- 1 cup (240 ml) unsweetened oatmilk, divided
- 1/3 cup (80 ml) peeled and well-cooked broken chestnuts
- 2 tablespoons raw honey

Instructions

1. Pour 1/3 cup (80 ml) of the oatmilk into the blender and add the chestnuts. Blend on high speed until the chestnuts are completely broken down and you have a thick, creamy consistency.
2. With the machine running, add the remaining oatmilk and the raw honey until all the ingredients are well blended. Serve gently warmed or chilled. Stored in the refrigerator in a covered container, Creamy Chestnut Milk will keep for up to 5 days.

Adapted from a recipe in "Vegetarians in Paradise -Chestnut Recipes"

Castagnaccio Latte (Italian Chestnut Milk)

This recipe dates back centuries and is rooted in Italian culinary traditions, particularly in the Tuscany region, where chestnuts were once considered the "bread of the poor."

Ingredients

- 200g chestnut flour (sweet chestnut flour)
- 500ml whole milk (use almond / oat milk for a vegan version)
- 2 tbsp honey or sugar (optional)
- A pinch of salt
- A sprinkle of cinnamon or a dash of vanilla extract (optional)

Instructions

1. In a saucepan, combine chestnut flour and milk, whisking to avoid lumps.
2. Heat the mixture over medium heat, stirring continuously until it begins to thicken (about 10 minutes).
3. If desired, add honey or sugar for sweetness, along with a pinch of salt.
4. Remove from heat and add cinnamon or vanilla extract to enhance flavor.
5. Serve warm, garnished with a cinnamon stick or a drizzle of honey.
6. This warm, creamy drink is known for its rich and nutty taste and has been enjoyed for generations, especially during cooler months.

Japanese Kurigohan Cha (Chestnut Rice Tea)

While not strictly a "drink," this infusion has historical roots in Japanese tea culture and utilizes chestnut rice, reflecting the deep ties between chestnut consumption and traditional East Asian practices.

Ingredients

- 6-8 roasted chestnuts (peeled)
- 1 cup cooked sticky rice (mochi rice)
- 4 cups water
- 1 tbsp green tea leaves (Sencha or Genmaicha recommended)
- 1 tsp honey or rice syrup (optional)

Instructions

1. Roast chestnuts and peel them, setting aside a few whole for garnish.
2. In a pot, add water and the peeled roasted chestnuts; bring to a gentle boil.
3. Once boiling, reduce to a simmer and add the cooked sticky rice.
4. Allow the mixture to infuse for about 10-15 minutes.
5. Strain the liquid into a teapot with green tea leaves; let it steep for another 2-3 minutes.
6. Serve warm in small tea cups, optionally sweetened with honey or rice syrup.
7. This tea reflects centuries of Japanese chestnut culture, combining earthy flavors with a hint of sweetness.

Traditional French Crème de Marrons Liqueur (Chestnut Liqueur)

A French classic, Crème de Marrons (sweet chestnut purée) has been a delicacy for centuries, particularly in regions like Ardèche.

Ingredients

- 250g roasted and peeled chestnuts
- 1 liter vodka or brandy
- 300g sugar
- 1 vanilla bean, split
- 500ml water

Instructions

1. Roast and peel the chestnuts, then roughly chop them.
2. In a large glass jar, combine the chestnuts with vodka or brandy, ensuring they are fully submerged.
3. Add the split vanilla bean to the mixture and seal the jar. Cool in a dark place for at least 4 weeks, shaking occasionally.
4. After 4 weeks, make a simple syrup by dissolving sugar in water over low heat.
5. Strain the chestnut-infused alcohol, discarding solids, and mix with the cooled syrup.
6. Bottle the liqueur and let it age for an additional 2 weeks. Serve chilled or over ice.
7. This traditional chestnut liqueur, rich with vanilla and sweet chestnut flavors, dates back hundreds of years in Europe.
8. Each recipe connects to a unique chestnut tradition, offering a glimpse into how different cultures

Spicy Chestnut and Cherry Nog

Yield: about 3 3/4 cups (900 ml)

Ingredients

- 2 cups (480 ml) oat milk, divided
- 2/3 cup (160 g) peeled and well-cooked broken chestnuts
- 1 cup fresh Cherries, pitted
- 1/2 cup (120 ml) maple syrup or raw honey
- 1 teaspoon vanilla extract
- 1/2 teaspoon ground cinnamon
- 1/2 teaspoon ground cardamom
- 1/2 teaspoon ground nutmeg
- 1/8 teaspoon ground cloves

Instructions

1. Pour 1 cup (240 ml) of the oat milk into the blender and add the chestnuts and fresh cherries. Blend on high speed until the chestnuts and cherries are completely broken down and you have a thick, creamy consistency.
2. With the machine running, add the remaining oat milk, maple syrup or honey, vanilla extract, and spices and blend for 30 seconds, or until all the ingredients are blended and foamy.
3. Serve immediately, or chill thoroughly. Stored in the refrigerator in a covered container, Spicy Chestnut and Cherry Nog will keep for up to 5 days.

Adapted from a recipe in "Vegetarians in Paradise -Chestnut Recipes"

Chestnuts and Beer

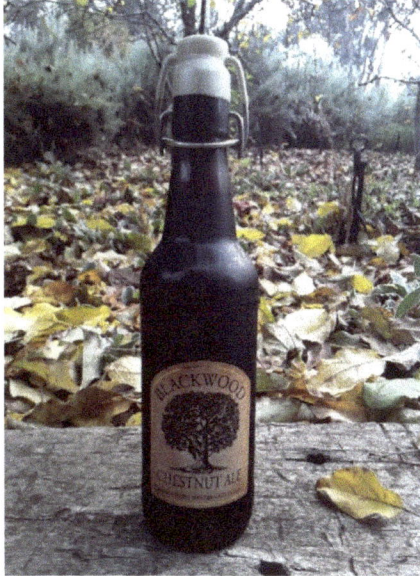

Chestnut Brae's Gold Medal Chestnut Ale

An Italian friend we talked to mentioned that chestnuts must be eaten with wine and not beer. He believes that the yeast in beer and the chestnuts combine and give you heart burn and a gaseous stomach...so that is probably why you do not see chestnuts served in an English pub.

Chestnut Ale however, is a popular drink in Corsica and ales are produced around the world. Our own chestnut ale is brewed by the Blackwood Valley Brewing Company and won the gold medal at the International Beer awards in Melbourne in June 2017 and 2021.

Chestnut Liqueur

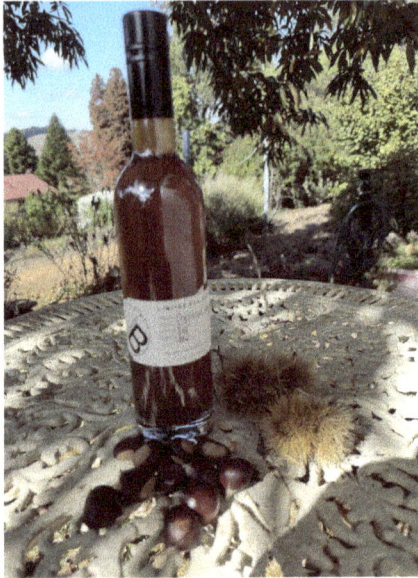

Chestnut Liqueur

We first heard about Chestnut Liqueur from the Alsace region of France. The liqueur is 18% alcohol and is a bewitching creamy, sweet taste which is ideal with cheese or ice cream. We started producing this liqueur with Blackwood Valley Brewing Company in December 2021 and it is now one of our top sellers.

About Chestnut Brae

Chestnut Brae is a 70 acre sweet chestnut farm in Nannup, Western Australia. The farm comprises 1000 sweet chestnut trees, a farmstay, a processing facility, a commercial kitchen, a mill room, and a farm shop. John and Linda Stanley run farm tours and events on the farm. For appointments email info@chestnutbrae.com.au, to purchase products online or to book tours or accommodation, visit **www.chestnutbrae.com.au.**

The farm is located at 106 McKittrick Road, Carlotta, Western Australia, 6275.

The postal address is PO Box 200, Nannup, Western Australia, 6275.

www.ingramcontent.com/pod-product-compliance
Lightning Source LLC
Chambersburg PA
CBHW041258040426
42334CB00028BA/3069